MAD MADAME LALAURIE

MAD MADAME LALAURIE

NEW ORLEANS' MOST FAMOUS MURDERESS REVEALED

VICTORIA COSNER LOVE +
LORELEI SHANNON

Charleston • London

THE
History
PRESS

Published by The History Press
Charleston, SC 29403
www.historypress.net

First published 2011

Manufactured in the United States

ISBN 978.1.60949.199.4

Library of Congress Cataloging-in-Publication Data

Love, Victoria Cosner.
  Mad Madame Lalaurie : New Orleans's most famous murderess revealed / Victoria Cosner
Love and Lorelei Shannon.
      p. cm.
  Includes bibliographical references.
  ISBN 978-1-60949-199-4
  1. Lalaurie, Delphine. 2. Women murderers--Louisiana--New Orleans--Biography. I.
Shannon, Lorelei. II. Title.
  HV6248.L1825L68 2010
  364.152'3092--dc22
  [B]
                                    2010052978

From Victoria Love—
This is dedicated to my family, who let me babble about death, torture, slavery and other horrors, and also to Lorelei, who always feeds my morbid soul.

From Lorelei Shannon—
For the victims of the Lalauries, the victims of Hurricane Katrina and for the beautiful city of New Orleans. And for Victoria. Thank you so much for trusting me to assist with this fascinating project.

Contents

Acknowledgements

V ictoria Love: Finding some of these documents, unveiling the secrets and methodically breaking down the legend was exhilarating and comes so rarely in a history buff's life. It was long past time to tell this story.

I want to thank my husband, Brian, who let me persist in this wild chase through history despite having a full-time job and two kids. He also translated our French documents and phrases for us. My mom got me numerous books from interlibrary loan at her local library despite the embarrassment of her having to pick up titles on serial-killing women, death, maiming and worse. The staffs of the Missouri Historical Society (St. Louis) and the Williams Research Center in New Orleans were stellar and patient with my questions and many requests. Ricardo Pustanio was more than gracious in sharing family history and his art. Claudia Williams and her staff provided patient answers to my zombie lore questions. Thank you to the staff of The History Press for their trust and patience, especially Becky Lejeune, Ryan Finn and Ashley Mancill. Thank you also to Fran Lawren and Pamela Bigelow for editing this complex history. I always wanted to thank my parents for not putting me in therapy when my interest in the morbid or macabre raised its head early in my life, so now is the time. And, of course, thanks to Lorelei, who took on the task with me of writing and editing this book. She inspires me every day.

L orelei Shannon: Thanks to my family for putting up with my obsessive interest in this book. Huge, gigantic, enormous thanks to Victoria Love for getting the research done with such thoroughness, flair and ingenuity. As usual, I'm in awe. Thanks to my dogs for letting me hug them when I'd get freaked out by the subject material of this book. I love you all.

Chapter 1
The Legend

Believe it or leave it, there are ghosts in the French Quarter's famous haunted house at 1140 Royal St.
—States Item, *March 7, 1966*

In the Rue Royale stands this quaint, old-fashioned house about which so much has been written, and around which cluster so many wild and weird stories, that even in its philosophic day, few in the old faubourg care to pass the place after nightfall, or, doing so, shudder and hurry on with bated breath, as though midnight ghouls and ghosts hovered near, ready to exercise a mystic spell over all who dare invade its uncanny precincts.
—Marie Puents, Daily Picayune, *March 13, 1892*

No visit to New Orleans is complete without a ghost tour. There are literally dozens available, in any theme you can imagine: pirates, vampires, hauntings, paranormal activity and more. New Orleans has it all. Perhaps the most famous destination for tours of the macabre is the Lalaurie Mansion.

On the corner of Royal and Governor Nicholls Streets stands what some people say is the most haunted house in America. Imagine you are standing in the twilight of a warm summer day, looking at the house, which casts a long, ominous shadow down the street. This neoclassical, three-story mansion—complete with the traditional enclosed New Orleans–style courtyard—is said to be the site of a truly horrific case of torture, medical atrocities and abuse. It has witnessed more than 175 years of hauntings, terror, blood-crazed mobs and sorrow. Its austere exterior hides the elegant oasis within. If not quite beautiful, the house is dignified. It harkens back to the days when Creole Louisiana was king and the refinement of the lady of the house was paramount to a family's social success.

Imagine you are looking at the mansion, but you are not alone. A tour guide stands next to you. The two of you stare at the house in silence for a moment. When the tour guide begins to speak, she tells you a story:

> *In 1832, Madame Lalaurie, daughter of a prominent Creole family, and her nondescript husband, Dr. Louis Lalaurie, bought this elegant mansion and held the seasons' most exquisite parties. Madame Lalaurie was the crème of Creole society, renowned for her beauty and grace. Born Marie Delphine Macarty, Madame Lalaurie was married twice to prominent men who mysteriously died, leaving Madame a very wealthy widow. Then Marie Delphine met the good doctor, who had recently completed medical school in Toulouse and immigrated to New Orleans.*
>
> *In the spring of 1832, a cloud covered the Lalaurie Mansion. Whispers of slave abuse buzzed through the city. Louisiana didn't work on the Puritan/British code of ethics for slaves, which allowed an owner free rein to punish or even kill her slaves. The Code Noir, a decree that defined the conditions of slavery in the French colonial empire, was still enforced in Louisiana at that time, and it offered some meager protection to those enslaved. The code specifically forbade torture, mutilation and sexual abuse. It allowed for "ordinary" punishments, like confinement, chaining and whipping.*

Your tour guide gives you a dark look. "Those rumors must have been bad," she says.

> *A young American lawyer who was boarding in the neighborhood heard these rumors. He went to the Lalaurie home to point out the section of the Code Noir that prohibited severe abuse. He left dazzled by Madame Lalaurie, by her charm and beauty, denying that anyone so lovely could ever be cruel.*
>
> *The whispers died down. Madame continued to entertain lavishly, with her two quiet, reserved daughters by her side. She was known to give the last of her wine to the servant behind her, whispering, "Take this; it will do you good." There was even a court record from the 1820s that showed she had freed one of her slaves after the death of her second husband. It didn't seem possible that such a woman was abusing her household staff. Some people*

said the ugly stories were started by nouveaux-arrivés Americans, jealous of the Creole elite—just a nasty attempt to spoil their social standing and bring the proud Creoles down a notch.

But in 1833, an unfortunate incident occurred. While combing Madame Lalaurie's hair, a young slave girl named Nina hit a tangle and sent Madame into a rage. Madame chased the girl through the house with a bullwhip, shrieking like a madwoman. Nina fled up the stairs to the top of the house, with a raging Madame close behind.

Your tour guide points to the third floor. In the gloom, the house seems to be leaning toward you. After a moment, your guide continues:

High on the roof, the girl lost her footing and fell to the courtyard below. Her body hit with a dull thud. Blood spread in a dark halo around the child's head. Eyewitnesses said that Madame just stared at the dead child for a moment and then turned and went back inside.

Minutes later, silent shapes emerged from the house and dragged the broken body away. Later that night, the sound of a shovel could be heard in the courtyard, digging a shallow grave near the well. Quiet sobs filled the night. Nina was a beloved daughter and grandchild.

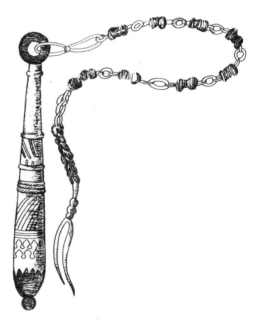

Bullwhips with metal or burned tips inflicted more pain on the victim.

The city wasn't blind. The witnesses summoned the police, and Madame was taken before a court of law. The judge was a relative, but New Orleans was watching. He couldn't let Madame off without some form of punishment. He fined her $300 and had her ten remaining slaves taken away from her. You would think that would be the end of that.

Your tour guide sadly shakes her head and continues:

It was only the beginning. Madame Lalaurie convinced another relative to secretly buy the slaves back for her.

There was no stopping the rumors after that horrible chain of events. It was said that Madame forced her gaunt and starved-looking slaves to serve her with their shirts off, men and women alike. Only her coach driver was reputed to "glow with health." He had to appear in public with Madame, after all. It wouldn't do for any aspect of her outward appearance to be less than perfect.

On April 10, 1834, an elderly female slave who was chained to the lit oven accidentally—or maybe deliberately—set the Lalaurie Mansion on fire. Flames consumed the kitchen and spread quickly to the main house, devouring antiques and art. A crowd gathered as friends and neighbors came to help.

Screaming was heard from the kitchen, and a face appeared in the window, an old slave shrieking for help—or maybe vengeance. "That woman is Nina's grandmother," someone whispered. "Somebody save her." It was too late—the woman was fully engulfed in flames.

"Where are the rest of the slaves?" one Good Samaritan asked Madame. "Never mind the slaves; save the valuables!" Madame responded coolly.

"Where are the slaves?" Judge Canongo, who lived nearby, asked Dr. Lalaurie. The doctor snapped, "Mind your own business and get to the task at hand."

Someone in the crowd yelled that the slaves were in the attic. Firemen went rushing up the stairs, where they encountered huge iron padlocks on the doors and smoke that choked their every breath.

"Where is the key?" demanded one of the would-be rescuers from above.

"Never mind that; take this painting out," was Madame Lalaurie's answer.

The firemen broke down the doors and found a scene more hellish than the inferno on the lower floors. These strong men, used to gore and carnage, backed out of the room shaking and retching. Some could not stop themselves from vomiting.

At last the firemen calmed themselves. Along with some of the Lalauries' neighbors, they went into the attic to save the poor wretched creatures they had discovered.

Everywhere the firemen looked, they saw chained slaves. Some were naked and some nearly dead. The stench of fear, sweat and human waste was stomach-turning, but what the firemen saw was infinitely worse.

Your guide lowers her voice, as if what she is about to say should never be repeated:

All of the slaves had been outrageously mutilated, abused or starved. One woman had her skin peeled in a spiral around and around her body, so she resembled a macabre caterpillar. One man and one woman appeared to have had a crude sex change operation performed on them. Her breasts were sloppily sewn onto his chest and his penis sewn to her crotch. Another man chained to the wall had a hole drilled into his head. Maggots crawled in and out of the open wound. A woman had all of her bones broken and reset at different angles, so that she resembled a nightmarish crab. When the doors burst open, she scuttled to a corner to hide, shrieking out a hideous, high-pitched barking sound. Buckets of body parts littered the room.

The tour guide pauses. Involuntarily, you shudder. After a moment, she continues.

Several of the slaves perished when rescuers tried to move them. Others fainted from the shock. One woman, blind with terror, jumped to her death from the window.

Leg iron shackles and the "ball and chain" were often used on slaves and prisoners.

15

The slaves were taken to the Cabildo, the massive building that served as the seat of colonial government in Spanish New Orleans and as the prison and slaveholding area for the American government. But they were not prisoners. They were taken to protect them from the howling, unpredictable mob. The stunned victims were placed in the slaveholding cells on the first level of the building. Local papers reported that more than four thousand people went to the Cabildo to see the "poor wretches" for themselves and to witness the cruelty the Lalauries had unleashed.

Meanwhile, Madame Lalaurie had retired to a portion of the house that was no longer in danger from the fire. Shortly after 6:00 p.m., her carriage arrived at the side door, as it did every evening. Her "sleek" driver, Bastien, opened the carriage door for her. Madame alighted for her evening ride, as she did every evening. The crowd could not believe their eyes. Madame Lalaurie waved to the mob as the carriage pulled away.

The rig rolled down Canal Street, toward the Bayou St. Jean, which emptied into Lake Pontchartrain, where the elite Creole often "took their air" in the evenings. Bayou St. Jean was also the location of the boat launch across Lake Pontchartrain.

"She's getting away, she's getting away!" roared the crowd. The mob pursued the carriage down Canal Street, but the horses were too fast. At the water's edge, Madame Lalaurie slipped from the carriage, her driver exchanged money with a pontoon captain and she boarded the boat.

The mob attacked and killed her horses and chopped her carriage into splinters. The fate of Bastien, the "sleek" driver, is unknown. One can only assume it was very unpleasant.

Illustration of a rockaway carriage similar to the one Madame Lalaurie used to escape the mob at her heels.

The tour guide leaves you to ponder this for a moment. You find you would rather not. The guide continues:

The details of Madame's escape are not known for certain, but on April 21, 1834, the Lalauries were in Mandeville, safely across Lake Pontchartrain, at the home of Louis Coquillon. Rumor had it that from Mandeville the Lalauries made their way to Mobile, where a ship took them to France.

The frustrated mob returned to the Lalaurie house and looted it, destroying anything that had not burned. The police struggled to keep the mob from setting the place ablaze again.

Policemen and firemen stayed on the scene for three weeks to keep vandals from razing the house to the ground. Policemen claimed to hear low moans and scratching sounds from the devastated building. They scoured the house, checking behind walls, but no additional victims could be found. The firefighters could find no more hidden rooms and no more experiments, but the noises continued. Police on the scene claimed that there were ghosts. The stories of hauntings had begun. There was no stopping the spread of the ghostly tales after that.

Looking up at the hulking mansion, you can easily imagine ghosts gliding through its halls. Your guide continues her story:

In the 1970s, renovations were started to divide the house into luxury apartments. Workmen pulled up the floors and discovered the bones of a dozen people who had been buried alive. This explained the cries and scratches the police had heard over 140 years before. The rescuers were so close, but they never knew that more victims lay right beneath their feet.

"And what happened to the Lalauries?" you ask, hoping for some kind of justice for these poor, murdered souls.

The Lalauries and their daughters disappeared. Most people think they fled to Paris. Some believe they never left Louisiana, while others have suggested that they went to Mobile. Wherever they ended up, neither Delphine Lalaurie nor her husband ever returned to New Orleans—not alive, anyway.

You briefly wonder what your guide meant by that, but she is speaking again.

There are two different stories of Madame's death. One is that she died amongst friends and family in 1842 in Paris. According to the other, more dramatic tale, Madame Lalaurie was recognized at a party in Paris, so she fled to Pau, France. There she was gored by a boar during a hunt. A fitting end for such a monster, if the story is true.

You find yourself nodding in agreement.

Following her death, Madame's body was secretly returned to New Orleans and buried in St. Louis Cemetery No. 1. One of the curates found a cemetery plaque with her name and death date in the cemetery's Alley No. 1. It's said that her descendants secretly visit her tomb.

You blink. You had visited the St. Louis Cemetery No. 1 earlier in the day. You saw voodoo queen Marie Laveau's tomb, but you had no idea that you were passing so close to the final resting place of a mass murderer as well. The tour guide resumes her story:

Despite the damage inflicted by the mob, the Lalaurie house has had many uses since its most notorious owners fled. It was a school for black and white girls during the Reconstruction era. This high-minded venture ended badly, with a mob coming in and physically removing the black girls from the school. For a while, the house was a music academy, but it was closed due to a public scandal. It was a furniture store, a bar called the Haunted Saloon, housing for Italian immigrants and a men's home called Warrington House.

Most of the owners reported paranormal incidents and a variety of specters. One man claimed to have seen a black man holding his head in his hands. Scrabbling, like the sound of a crab, has been heard in the attic over and over again.

Throughout the years, neighbors have reported the mansion's windows opening and closing by themselves and the front door opening with no human assistance. Moans, screams, a woman standing over sleeping occupants with a whip and a child tugging on sleeves have all been reported. Madame's fury at the slave child and the child's gory death are said to play out in their entirety for horrified spectators. The furniture store had to close because the furniture was repeatedly ripped during the night and found coated with some sort of unidentified goo in the morning. The owner waited up one night, thinking that vandals were responsible for the damage.

Illustration from Jeanne
DeLavigne's book.

He saw nothing and no one, but the next morning the furniture was ruined
again. He closed the store that day for the last time.

The guide turns toward you. You can see the glitter of her dark eyes in the
fading light. She continues:

Jeff Dwyer, author of The Ghost Hunter's Guide to New Orleans,
says that ghost hunters have the best chance to glimpse paranormal activity
by observing the mansion from the far side of Governor Nicholls Street,
where we are standing now.

You and the guide stare at the house for a long moment. You start when she begins to speak again:

> *The house was restored and divided into luxury apartments—that's when the bodies beneath the floors were discovered. Most recently it was bought by actor Nicolas Cage, who at one time owned at least three haunted houses in the New Orleans area, including Anne Rice's former residence in the Garden District. The Lalaurie house is currently on the market, for a sale price of $3.9 million. Care to buy it?*

The tour guide grins at you. You let out a nervous laugh. It is nearly dark outside. Windows inside the mansion are illuminated with a dull yellow light. You stare at the house and wonder. Is it haunted? An entire city seems to think so, and no house deserves to be haunted more than the Lalaurie Mansion.

What you've just heard is the stuff of New Orleans legend. But how much of the legend is grounded in fact, and how much is the result of sensational journalism, nearly two centuries of gossip and the embellishments of the tourism industry?

If you want to know the real story of Madame Lalaurie, turn the page. Her story is deep and complex, and shocking new twists have been unearthed. Discover the truth for yourself, if you dare.

Chapter 2
Delphine's Early Life and First Marriage

Your petition, whatever it is, is granted, you are so beautiful!
—María Luisa of Parma (1751–1819), Queen of Spain, to Marie Delphine Macarty López

D elphine Lalaurie has always been a mystery. Her early life is not well documented, and there is no reason to expect that it should be. Delphine Macarty was born into a wealthy, prolific New Orleans family in about 1775. Her family boasted a mayor, a governor, three chevaliers of the French Crown, ousted Irish nobility, several slave traders and some of the most gracious, renowned hostesses of eighteenth-century New Orleans.

If there had been any hint in her childhood of her dark future, her parents would have kept it well hidden. Likewise, if Delphine had been abused in some way that affected her development, it would have been the darkest of secrets. The only certainty is that she was a beautiful child. Tales of her beauty and charm followed her throughout her life.

Her father, Barthélémy Louis de Macarty, married Madame Marie Jeanne Lovable (Widow Lacompte), and the two started a family: two sons, Jean Baptiste François and Barthélémy Louis, and their uncommonly beautiful daughter, Marie Delphine.

Delphine grew up in a typical wealthy Creole household. The family owned a plantation north of the city and a house in the Vieux Carré in the growing Faubourg St. Marie suburb. Delphine appears to have been a happy, sociable girl. Neighbors told of her gracious visits to their plantations. The Macarty plantation was a popular spot for dignitaries and despots visiting the blossoming New Orleans. Delphine would have been introduced

St. Louis Cathedral, where
Delphine and Don Ramón López
were married.

to many people of high station, giving her plenty of practice refining her manners and charm.

As the daughter of a well-bred Creole family, she would have been taught to read and write, but the bulk of her education probably consisted of music, art lessons and etiquette. She would have learned the art of running a household from her mother.

Creole girls were introduced to society at the age of fifteen and were often married by sixteen or seventeen. For some reason lost to history, Delphine didn't marry until she was about twenty-four. It can be surmised that either her late marriage wasn't late at all—her year of birth was listed incorrectly after all—or perhaps it had something to do with her affluent aunts waiting until an appropriate prize could be found for their beautiful niece. Her first husband was a prominent and controversial figure in the Spanish-controlled colonial government of Louisiana.

On January 1, 1800, the new intendant of Louisiana, Don Ramón López y Angulo, took office. Most likely introduced by her influential aunt, Céleste Miró (wife of Governor Miró), Delphine married Don Ramón, Cabellero pensionado de la real y distinguida Orden espanola de Carlos III of Spain, on June 11, 1800. They were wed in the St. Louis Cathedral, with her parents as witnesses.

Little is known about the details of their marriage or the true character of Don Ramón López. However, a variety of correspondence between López and Charles de Hault Delassus, the last Spanish lieutenant governor of Upper Louisiana, exists in the St. Vrain Collection of the Missouri History Museum's archives. In his writings, López shows himself to be very thrifty, always worried about money. At one point, he makes a request to have the slave trade opened back up in the Louisiana territory due to lack of paid manpower to keep the crops, and thus the money flow, moving: "Don Raymond de López y Angulo…having decided to suspend on his behalf the existing prohibition on the importation of Negro slaves, due to extenuating circumstances in the colony."

This request was denied, and his frustration with the lack of funds continued to fester. On the surface, he seemed to be a man who was deeply invested in his job. However, a Louisiana historian, Arthur Preston Whitaker cited that López's papers were in "utter confusion" when he left his position of intendant of New Orleans in 1801, due mostly to lack of interest in his position.

López was a knight pensioner of the royal and distinguished order of Charles III, according to author Charles Gayerré. He married Delphine without the consent of the king of Spain, which was against the government's protocol yet was a path that several other Spanish officers in Louisiana had pioneered. Why a man who already considered himself in his government's bad graces would have made such a rash decision is somewhat baffling. It is easy to romanticize the situation and speculate that he was so taken with Delphine's beauty and charm that he could not resist her. Or perhaps her family's finances and power were too good to pass up. His actual reasons will never be known, but he paid dearly for his choice.

López was stripped of his office and ordered to return to the Spanish court. López pleaded extenuating circumstances and precedents set by Governors Unzaga, Galvez and Miró (who married Delphine's aunt); by his predecessor, acting intendant Morales; and by Minister Irujo of Philadelphia. The bishop of Louisiana tried to intercede as well, but to no avail, according to author Arthur Whitaker. He was exiled to San Sebastian, on the northern coast of Spain, near the French border.

In the fall of 1801, Don Ramón de López y Angulo surrendered his office into the hands of Don Juan Ventura Morales, who was to fulfill his functions

Illustration of Iglesia del Espirito in Havana, Cuba, the probable burial place of Ramón López.

ad interim, and prepared to depart for Spain. But, in settling his accounts, it seems he got into serious difficulties with his successor, who brought an accusation against him before the Spanish ministry. In answer to it, López complained bitterly of Morales, who, he said, threw in his way interminable delays and litigation on the clearest and most insignificant points and on grounds that were unfounded and unjust, as Gayerré noted. "Wherefore," he continued, "considering that the crafty and intense malignity of Morales and of his satellite, the assessor [Serano] who is also my mortal enemy, know no bounds, I again beg your Excellency [the minister in Spain] to suspend your decision."

In 1800, Spain ceded Louisiana back to France, but the Spanish government still held a strong presence in the territory. In 1803, the United States took possession of Louisiana from France with the famous Louisiana Purchase. On March 26, 1804, Don Ramón de López y Angulo was pardoned by the Spanish government. He was again granted a government position in New Orleans. Historians believe that while en route to Louisiana via the American ship *Ulysses* López died of heart failure, probably on a stopover in Havana, Cuba.

There are two stories told about the end of this chapter of Delphine's life. One is that López was called back to Spain to serve King Charles IV, but he died along the way, leaving behind a pregnant Delphine. His lovely bride was widowed and gave birth on the same unfortunate trip.

The other story is one of a dutiful wife coming to the aid of her wronged husband. According to this story, told by author Elizabeth King,

> [Delphine] *was a woman of such great beauty that when she went to Spain to solicit the protection of the Queen of Spain for her husband, who had incurred a military punishment, she did no more than kneel in a garden where the Queen took her morning walk. Her long black hair was unbound and hanging about her shoulders, her lovely eyes raised in supplication. The Queen stopped at sight of her, so young and so beautiful, and approached her with the words: "Your petition, whatever it is, is granted, you are so beautiful!"*

After successfully advocating for her husband's cause, Delphine returned to Cuba (a common stop on the way from Louisiana to Europe), only to learn that López was already dead. Delphine's daughter was born on the return trip back from Spain, but whether it was aboard the ship or in Havana is unclear. The historical records are contradictory.

Named Marie Françoise de Boya de López y Angulo, Delphine's daughter was noted for her beauty and was nicknamed "Borquita," a diminutive form of her great-grandmother's name. Borquita, educated in Europe, would eventually marry into the Forstall family, and her twelve children would establish a New Orleans and Louisiana dynasty.

Chapter 3
Delphine's Second Marriage

A few less scrupulous New Orleans merchants such as Jean Blanque, engaged sailors who plied both sides of the law.

—historian William C. Davis

In 1808, Delphine, now about thirty-two years of age and with an eight-year-old daughter, married a man named Jean Blanque.

Jean Pierre Paulin Blanque, native of Béarn, France, came to Louisiana with Prefect Laussat in 1803. He was reputed to be an important man in New Orleans commerce and politics. The 1805 New Orleans Directory listed Jean Blanque as living at 24 Rue St. Louis with two other males over sixteen years of age, as well as two slaves. Historian Edward Larocque Tinker described him as having "dark hair and eyes, an oval face and [was a] noted orator."

Jean Blanque bought a "two story brick house, almost completed," and designed by the prominent architect Dujarreau in 1808. The Blanques resided at 409 Royal Street (now Ida Manheim Antiques) and, according to legend, maintained a home outside of town called Ville Blanque. Although this other home has not been located, King described it: "In that stylish Royal Street home or in the 'Villa Blanque,' a charming country place fronting the Mississippi River just below the city limits, Delphine Macarty Blanque divided her time, both places frequented by the socially elect."

Louisiana historian Henry C. Castellanos noted that

> [h]er reunions were recherché affairs, and during the lifetime of her former husband, Mr. Jean Blanque, who figures so conspicuously in Louisiana's

The Creole socialites and political leaders of the day raved of Madame Blanque's entertainment at the Blanque House on Royal Street. *Photo by Victoria Cosner Love.*

legislative history, and whose important services to the State during the long series of years should be gratefully remembered, her home was the resort of every dignitary in the infancy of our state. There the politicians of the period met on neutral ground, eschewing for the nonce their petty jealousies, cabals and intrigues to join in scenes of enjoyment and refinement: among whom I may cite Claiborne, the Governor; Wilkinson, the military commander; Trudeau, the Surveyor General, Bosque, Marigny, Destrehan, Sauve, Derbigny, Macarty, de la Ronde, Villere and other all representatives of the "ancient regime."

The Blanques had four children: Marie Louise Jeanne (born 1810); Louise Marie Laure (born 1811); Jean Pierre Paulin (born 1815); and Marie Louise

Pauline (born 1816). Delphine's daughter from her previous marriage, Borquita, also lived in this household until she married. On the surface, Delphine and her family appeared to be living the respectable, genteel life of an upper-class Creole family. But where Jean Blanque's money came from was a different matter entirely.

Historian Arthur Clisby, in his book *Old New Orleans*, described Jean Blanque:

> *Jean Blanque, once a well-known figure in old New Orleans. Merchant, lawyer, banker, legislator, and—this was told in whispers—the "man higher up" in certain transactions relative to the importation of "black ivory" and goods upon which customs duties were not collected. M. Blanque earned this distinction during the hectic days before the Battle of New Orleans was fought, when the slave smuggling activities of a swaggering company of Baratarians under the leadership of Pierre and Jean Laffite, sometimes designated as pirates were at their height. It will be remembered that it was to Jean Blanque that Jean Laffite sent his letters exposing the attempt of the British emissaries to seduce the Baratarians to the English cause prior to the appearance of the British invading army in 1815.*

Blanque comes up more than 350 times in the slave schedules, listed as buying and selling slaves. It was widely known that he owned boats used in privateering. He was on the New Orleans City Council, but his main claim to fame seems to have been that Jean Laffite, the famous pirate, wrote to him for assistance when Laffite was negotiating with the American army to help them with the Battle of New Orleans, according to Gayerré:

> *These two letters of John (Jean, ed.) Lafitte the younger were forwarded to their destination by Pierre Lafitte, the elder, who had found the means not to remain long in the jail where he was incarcerated in New Orleans, and who added to the package this note to Blanque: "On my arrival here, I was informed of all the occurrences that have taken place. I think I may justly commend my brother's conduct under such difficult circumstances. I am persuaded he could not have made a better choice than in making you the depositary of the papers that were sent to us, and which may be of great importance to the State. Being fully determined to follow the plan that may reconcile us with the Government, I herewith send you a letter directed to his Excellency the Governor, which I submit to your discretion to deliver, or not, as you may think proper. I have not yet been honored with an answer from*

New Orleans' Most Famous Murderess Revealed

William C. Davis described Jean Blanque as one of "a few less scrupulous New Orleans merchants…[who] engaged sailors who plied both sides of the law." It was alleged that Blanque was the consignee of the cargo of "Captain Lafitte's" prize British merchantman Hector, revealed later to be an impostor smuggling goods under forged ship's papers. In 1806, Blanque was taken to federal court for purchasing twenty-seven thousand pounds of illegally obtained coffee. Although many merchants were attracted to the low prices and the variety of the goods being sold by pirates, Blanque's purchases attracted enough attention to have him taken to court, according to Davis.

To add more to the man's mystique, he was the same Jean Paul Blanque, the commissioner of war under Napoleon, who came to Louisiana as a public servant of the country of France with Louisiana's last French governor, Prefect Pierre Clement de Laussat. Laussat's wicked sense of humor and great storytelling abilities make his memoirs an enjoyable read. From these memoirs, a little of Blanque's personality emerges. In 1804, Blanque was sent by Laussat to attend the meetings with Clairborne and General Wilkenson during the transfer of the Louisiana Territory to America, so he must have been a man of some influence.

Blanque was noted for his strong oratory skills and hot temper. Laussat recounts a story in which Blanque physically removed a man from Laussat's presence, presumably due to some insult. Blanque also wrote a twenty-four-page treatise in retaliation against a political opponent's treatise directed at Laussat. Emotional phrases, including references to "Don Quixote" and "tilting at windmills," highlighted the booklet that Blanque self-published and distributed throughout the Vieux Carré. (The booklet is available for viewing at the Williams Research Center.)

Blanque and Company was used by Laussat as a commercial house for financial transactions for the French government. In Laussat's personal papers, at least six transactions are noted, with a 10 percent fee paid per transaction—quite a handy business to have waiting for you in a new country.

As New Orleans grew, so did Jean Blanque's role in a variety of offices and organizations. Officers to a new Masonic lodge were elected in June 1812. The officers were installed on July 11, 1812. At that time, the "Grand Convention of Ancient York Rite Masons met in Perfect Union Lodge Room and elected the following Officers…and Jean Blanque, Worshipful Master of Charity Lodge," according to the lodge history in Gayerré's book.

Gayerré's *History of Louisiana* made reference to Blanque's considerable influence:

> *One of Blanque's political adversaries, Colonel Declouet certainly found himself in a very critical situation. According to Duncan's and Davezac's testimony, which is given at length in the report of the Committee of Investigation, he had accused the Legislature of treason; he had accused Guichard, the Speaker of the House, Blanque, Marigny and others who always voted with Blanque, a very influential member of the House, of being at the head of the movement. He had asserted that Guichard had attempted to obtain his co-operation by telling him that General Jackson made war after the Russian fashion, which was to destroy everything rather than give up the possession of the country to the British, whilst the enemy would respect property. Major Tully Robinson and Major Tessier also swore that Declouet had mentioned to them, Blanque, Guichard and Marigny as using their influence in the Legislature to dispose that body to a capitulation, in order to prevent the destruction of property, "which should not be sacrificed to military pride."*
>
> *By the majority, he explained that he meant such members as always voted with Blanque, and composed the French side of the House, with the exception of Rouffignac and Louaillier, who sometimes dissented. He believed that the men he named had sufficient influence to control and lead the Legislature as they wished. Such was, in substance, Davezac's testimony.*

On December 15, 1812, Blanque introduced into the House of Representatives this short, spirited address to the citizens of the state of

The Macarty plantation, headquarters to General Andrew Jackson during the War of 1812. This plantation was owned by Delphine's wealthy, unmarried aunt, Jeanne. It is no longer standing, despite its national significance.

Louisiana. Blanque's motive was to engage the populace in the protection of their newly adopted United States of America, as the British were planning an invasion of New Orleans. To that date, the primarily French Creole population had not stepped up to defend the city, shunning the American army. Blanque's words, again in Gayerré's work, moved them to action:

> *Your country is in danger; the enemy is at your doors; the frontiers of the State are invaded. Your country expects of you the greatest efforts to repulse the bold enemy who threatens to penetrate, in a few days, to the very hearthstones of your homes; the safety of your persons, that of your property, of your wives and children, yet depends on you. Rush to arms, fellow-citizens, enlist promptly under the banner of General Jackson, of that brave chief who is to command you; give him all your confidence; the successes he has already obtained assure you that to march under his standards is to march to victory. There is no longer any alternative; dear fellow-citizens, we must defend ourselves; we must conquer, or we must be trampled under the feet of a cruel and implacable enemy, whose known excesses will be as nothing when compared with those which he will perpetrate in our unfortunate country. To arms! Let us precipitate ourselves upon the enemy; let us save from his cruelty, from his barbarous outrages all that is dear to us, all that can bind us to life. Your Representatives have supplied the Executive with all the pecuniary means which he required of them for the defence [sic] of the State, and they will give you the example of the devotion which they expect of you.*

Jean Blanque died or disappeared in 1818, leaving Delphine with four children to raise. He also left his wife with plenty of money to live in style. Unfortunately, there is no documentation of his precise date of death. It is not known if he died without a will, but the parish court index cites about a dozen matters of his estate dealt with by Delphine after Jean Blanque's death. This lack of verification or notice in the papers is especially frustrating; there is no reason that his death would not have been documented—unless, perhaps, he was on the run from the law, had fled New Orleans or simply vanished to escape the shadier aspects of his past.

In July 1819, the records of the parish court show Marie Delphine Macarty, widow of the late John Blanque, presenting an emancipation petition to the court noting that she "intends to emancipate" her male slave named Jean Louis, "of upwards of fifty years of age." She declares that Jean Louis has always "led an honest conduct," has not run away and has not committed any crime. Marie Delphine Macarty Blanque asked the court to order that the "notices prescribed by law" be published in the "usual place and form" in order to enable her to emancipate her slave. This is an interesting action for a woman who later appears to revel in the suffering of her slaves.

Delphine Blanque seems to have thrived in her marriage to the rich, influential and handsome Jean Blanque. The Blanques' Royal Street residence, a grand mansion with twenty-four-foot ceilings, and their hideaway outside the city were alive with balls and outings during their union. The Macarty women were still in their heyday, and Delphine's position in New Orleans was that of a rising star.

There is no record of what Delphine thought about Jean Blanque's alleged pirating and smuggling activities, but she and her children blossomed while she was with him and, thanks to his fortune, did quite well after his unexpected demise/disappearance.

Was it exciting for Delphine to be married to such a volatile man? Did she relish the stories of his exploits or ignore them? She was married to Jean Blanque for many years, and they were parted only by death or his abrupt departure. Whether theirs was a true love story, and whether Delphine enjoyed being the wife of an outlaw or just enjoyed the financial benefits it brought, remains a mystery.

Bird's-eye view of New Orleans, Louisiana, with the Mississippi River in the foreground, circa 1851. *Printed by J. Bachman (Bachmann), Library of Congress Panoramic Maps (2nd ed.), 240.1.*

Chapter 4
Louis Lalaurie and the "Catastrophe of 1834"

XXXVIII. We also forbid all our subjects in this colony, whatever their condition or rank may be, to apply, on their own private authority, the rack to their slaves, under any pretense whatever, and to mutilate said slaves in any one of their limbs, or in any part of their bodies, under the penalty of the confiscation of said slaves; and said masters, so offending, shall be liable to a criminal prosecution. We only permit masters, when they shall think that the case requires it, to put their slaves in irons, and to have them whipped with rods or ropes.
—Louisiana Code Noir, 1724

On January 12, 1828, Delphine married Leonard Louis Nicolas Lalaurie, MD, who had arrived from France on February 13, 1825. Louis' birth date estimates range from 1771 to 1800, but he was supposed to have been somewhat younger than Delphine. He was born in Villeneuve-sur-Lot in Aquitaine, not far from the home of Delphine's second husband, Jean Blanque, nor from San Sabastion, where her first husband, López, was exiled.

Lalaurie was a mediocre medical student who eventually graduated from dental school in Toulouse. After graduation, Lalaurie prepared to immigrate to Louisiana. Dozens of letters to Louis from his father, François Jean Lalaurie, provide insight into their relationship. Often nagging, François wrote to his son every two weeks, mostly inquiring about his completion of his application to the Friends of the Bourbons (Masonic) organization. This collection, housed with the Missouri Historical Society, also contains several letters to Louis from his sisters. He seems to have had warm, affectionate relationships with Victoire, Rosalie and Helene. There is no indication in his letters that Louis lacked respect for women—or that he would eventually become an abusive husband.

Louis Lalaurie kept a detailed journal of the weather conditions on his journey across the Atlantic to New Orleans. He left on the boat *Fanny* on December 8, 1824, and arrived on February 13, 1825. His writing is dry. The journal shows that the doctor had an eye for scientific detail, but little personality emerges from his meticulous notes. The translation is located in the Delassus–St. Vrain Collection at the Missouri History Museum Archives in St. Louis. It is a painful read, even for the most avid of history fans. One month after his arrival, Dr. Lalaurie sought to establish a medical practice in New Orleans. An intriguing tidbit was cited in Rudolph Matas's *History of Medicine in Louisiana*:

> *By 1825, too, surgical developments in England and France were rapidly finding their way to Louisiana. An advertisement in the form of a letter to the editor appeared in the Courier on March 18* [Matas then quotes Lalaurie]*:*

> *"I pray you to announce in your next number that a French Physician has just arrived in this city, who is acquainted with the means, lately discovered in France, of destroying Hunches. The individual submitting to the operations required, sees his deformity gradually diminish, and after a treatment longer or shorter, according to the extent of the deformity, the body resumes its natural forms. That discovery has met with the greatest success in France, and everything induces the belief that it will have the same result in this country."*

Matas asserted that Dr. Lalaurie sounded "quite different from the blatant appeals of the obvious quacks." Lalaurie's "[p]ossession of a license from the Comte Medicale" indicated that Lalaurie had graduated from an accredited French medical school. He also pointed out that Lalaurie did not intend to restrict himself to just one area of medicine.

As an interesting aside, the practice of medicine was almost unregulated in the early 1800s. It wasn't unusual for doctors who studied one specialty to randomly switch to another, as Louis Lalaurie did.

By September 1827, Delphine Macarty López Blanque and Dr. Lalaurie were acquainted enough for her to send a small handwritten note to Lalaurie requesting a personal favor (translated by Brian Love):

New Orleans' Most Famous Murderess Revealed

Messr. Lalaurie, I ask Mr. Lalaurie to have the courtesy to seal and address these letters and send them to Mademoiselle Pauline. Having a letter without an address, Monsieur St. Avid had supposed it would be for him. The "Mandizes" leaves today. I would ask if your business permits to throw them in the bag. Pauline has been sick, I pray that you will kindly take this responsibility and excuse my indiscretion. Blanque nee Macarty.

This is an intriguing historical tidbit. It meant enough to Dr. Lalaurie to entrust the note to his lawyer/son-in-law, Auguste Delassus. Additionally, it indicates a relationship of some sort—Lalaurie seems to know where Pauline, Delphine's daughter, was living. But the note has an oddly formal tone considering that the couple would be married three months later, in early 1828. Their son, Jean Louis, would be born later that same year.

Louis and Delphine bought the mansion at 1140 Rue Royal in 1832, four years into their marriage. The mansion, a beautiful two-story Creole-style building with an interior courtyard and several balconies to allow the air to circulate through the house, had been built in 1831. The Lalauries had the mansion opulently decorated and filled with gorgeous furniture and fine art. The couple threw lavish parties, which were often written up in the society pages.

Delphine Lalaurie was one of the sparkling queens of Creole high society. Often overlooked and deemed by many to be reserved, Louis Lalaurie was overshadowed by his gorgeous wife.

There is no documentation of Dr. Lalaurie having an established medical practice in New Orleans during this time. However, in the Delassus–St. Vrain Collection at the Missouri Historical Society (MHS) there is a variety of receipts and written requests for Dr. Lalaurie's services. One acquaintance wrote to Lalaurie for assistance with a slave who was ailing, and Lalaurie billed him for a potion. (It's worth noting that slaves were often test subjects for doctors' untried potions and remedies. This practice was not uncommon or considered unethical.) Another client asked for a tooth removal. Lalaurie was obviously working from his home, which also was not unusual for the time.

Curiously, Dr. Lalaurie is often left mostly out of the accounts of the atrocities found in his house in 1834. He is occasionally mentioned as a co-perpetrator and, more often, as a background figure, paling in the shadow of his wife's overpowering evil. However, for the sake of argument, if some of the horrors the slaves endured were, in fact, medical experiments, who would have been more likely to commit them? A society belle (no matter how cruel)…or her physician husband?

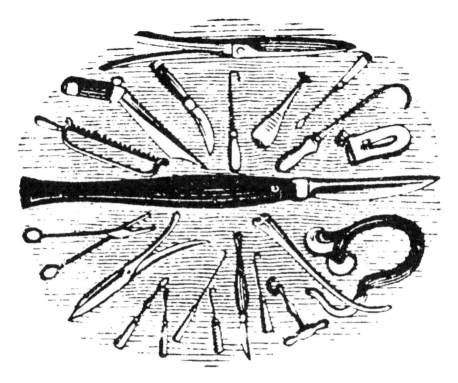

Sordid rumors of medical experiments and zombie drugs dogged the Lalauries.

A doctor studying physical deformities makes a likely suspect when medical experiments are discovered under his very roof. No proof that the medical experiments actually took place exists. However, Dr. Louis Lalaurie has some interesting myths circulating around him in his own right.

New Orleans artist Ricardo Pustanio, famous for his paintings of Madame Lalaurie and the "Devil Baby" of Bourbon Street, stated in an interview with the authors that some New Orleans natives believe that Dr. Lalaurie was testing Haitian-style "zombie drugs" to try to induce cooperation and docility in troublesome slaves. He had many failures, and those poor, poisoned souls were said to have been thrown into the swamp. This bizarre theory is discussed in more detail in the tenth chapter.

Dr. Lalaurie has also been associated with the Devil Baby. This was supposedly a deformed or insane child, rumored to be the spawn of a mortal woman and a demon; the baby was found by voodoo queen Marie Laveau and given to Delphine and Louis Lalaurie to raise. This, too, is discussed in the tenth chapter.

No portraits survive of Louis Lalaurie. It can be assumed if any were made that they were destroyed during the 1834 fire or the riot that followed. What would such a man have looked like? A man, often described as nondescript, who somehow managed to woo and marry one of the most beautiful and richest widows in New Orleans? A man who was guilty of, or at least complicit in, the most shocking atrocities New Orleans had ever seen? It's doubtful that his formal portrait would have revealed much of his inner nature, but we will never know.

The Lalauries lived a life of beauty and elegance, interrupted only briefly by rumors of slave abuse in the spring of 1832. Strangely, on October 26, 1832, the Lalauries petitioned the court to free their slave, "Devince, a Creole of Louisiana of about forty or forty five years of age." Their petition was granted in August 1833. Eight months later, the two would be revealed as torturers and, possibly, murderers of slaves.

On November 16, 1832, a summons was issued to Louis Lalaurie, residing in Plaquemines parish. Madame Lalaurie petitioned for separation from Louis, who was not living at the Royal address at that time. She cited that "through a series of ill treatment from the said Louis Lalaurie that indeed the said Lalaurie acted toward her a long time since in such a manner as to render their living together insupportable."

Madame Lalaurie swore that

> on the 26th of October last, in the presence of many witnesses, the said Louis Lalaurie went so far as to not only ill treat her but was to beat and wound her in the most outrageous and [illegible] manner. Wherefore, the plaintiff prays your honor to authorize her to sue her said husband for a separation from bed and board and thence forth to grant her decreed that they be separated from bed and board to authorize her to live separately in the meanwhile from her said husband.

Delphine asked the court to let her remain at the house at Royal and Hospital Streets. Judge Joshua Lawn signed an order allowing her to sue her husband for legal separation.

Note the date of the alleged incident of the beating—it is the same day on which the Lalauries were recorded as petitioning the court for the freedom of their slave Devince. The significance of this coincidence is somewhat baffling. Did the couple fight over Devince? Or did that date come to Madame's mind in her deposition because it was the day she had the man freed? Anyone who might have known the answer is long dead.

There is no record of Madame Lalaurie going forward with the case against her husband. But something unpleasant must have occurred between them. Delphine must have been strongly motivated to bring a case of spousal abuse before the court. After all, such allegations did not go with her façade of domestic perfection, but it is unlikely that Delphine Lalaurie was a woman who would passively tolerate the role of abused wife.

If Louis Lalaurie was, in fact, habitually abusing Delphine, one has to question who was the monster in this tragic and horrifying story.

In another somewhat odd incident, Madame Lalaurie lent money to a free woman of color, Sarah Lee, in 1833. Delphine would later sue Sarah Lee, from her exile in Paris, for the recovery of the loan in 1835. The lawsuit ended in 1840, awarding Madame Lalaurie the money that she was due.

Did the initial loan indicate that Madame Lalaurie was not averse to people of color? Quite possibly. But the abuse of the slaves in the Lalaurie house probably had little to do with their color. They were there, they were available and they were helpless against a system that considered them possessions. It was the ultimate crime of opportunity, and it would be exposed to the world in the spring of 1834.

The house fire that began on April 10, 1834, changed the Lalauries' world. Often in the recounting of the story, Dr. Lalaurie is said to have been missing or even dead at the time of the fire. However, the deposition given by Judge Canongo in court on April 12, 1834, was printed in the *New Orleans Bee* on the same day:

AUTHENTIC PARTICULARS
The following deposition stating the material facts attendant upon the horrible disclosures at the late conflagration has been made by Judge Canongo before a magistrate—coming from the source it does, it is entitled to full credence. We shall make no comment, but let the document speak for itself.

State of Louisiana
City of New Orleans
Before Judge Preval

The Deponent declares that on Thurs. 10th, a fire took place on the premises of Mds. Lalaurie, that he repaired {rather?} as a citizen for the purpose of affording any assistance within his power; that on arriving, there he was apprised of there being in one of the apartments some slaves who were chained, and who were, from their situation, exposed to perish in the conflagration. That at first, he hesitated to speak to Mr. Lalaurie, but addressed some of the friends of the family upon the subject. That seeing, however, all the persons present apparently indifferent to the result, he determined upon addressing both Mr. and Madame Lalaurie, who replied to his inquiries of the truth of what has been alleged, that it was slander. That he thereupon felt constrained to make fresh inquiries into the truth of what he had heard. That Messrs. Montreuil and Fernandez were near him, and he desired them both to go into the garret to make the necessary search, observing that he himself had attempted to do so, but was almost suffocated by the smoke. That these gentlemen had come to him some time after and had told him they had made a regular search but had found nobody. That a gentleman he believed to be Mr. Felix Lefebrve, came to him and said he had broke the bars of one of the apartments and he had discovered some slaves, intimating at the time his willingness to point out the place. That accompanied by several persons he reached the spot pointed out, and that it deemed advisable that the doors which were locked should be broken open. It was accordingly done. That he entered, accompanied by the citizens with him, two negresses were found incarcerated whom he liberated from this den as it were. That several voices were heard that there were other victims in the kitchen, that he repaired thither, but found no one. That one of the negresses had an iron collar, very large and very heavy, and was chained with heavy irons by the feet. That she walked with the greatest difficulty that he was unable to examine the one behind. That one individual, whom he believes to be Mr. Guillotte, said to him he knew of another slave was confined. That he entered with this gentleman into another apartment, where, upon someone's removing a mosquitoe bar, an old negress was found with a deep wound in her head. That she appeared to be quite feeble, too much so to be able to walk, that the deponent desired some of the persons present to have her removed to the mayor's office, where the first two had been removed. That upon his (deponent) demanding of Mr. Lalaurie if he had any slaves in his garret, he replied in an insulting tone, "that there were persons who would do much better by remaining at home than visiting others to dictate to them laws in the quality of officious friends."

This is not exactly the horror show of medical atrocities that the story would eventually evolve into, but it is certainly horrible enough. And it provides an eyewitness to Dr. Lalaurie's presence at the fire and his disregard of the helpless people perishing in his house. The story was

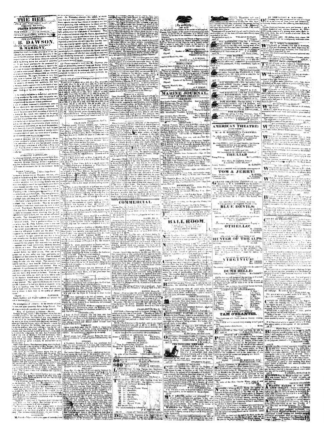

The April 12, 1834 edition of the *Bee* newspaper, with its ongoing coverage of the fire and its discoveries.

ghastly enough to drive the Lalauries, despite their wealth and social standing, out of the country.

Louis' character would be further tarnished early in the couple's exile. Madame and Dr. Lalaurie went to stay for a time at his family's estate in France. Madame's son, Paulin, later wrote a letter to his brother-in-law, Delassus, in which he spoke of the bad treatment that his mother Delphine received at the Lalauries' house. He referred to his stepfather's family as "those riff raff Lalauries" and mentioned that Dr. Louis Lalaurie was present during the alleged incidents of cruelty against Delphine. Paulin told his father that Delphine was "forced to lie without a bed" and went on to call the Lalauries *jean-foutre*, or jackasses.

Louis then disappeared from history for a while, and the Lalauries separated at some point. The last correspondence recorded from Louis Lalaurie was from Cuba in 1842, well before Delphine's newly established death date. (See the sixth chapter.) He wrote to Auguste Delassus, his son-in-law by marriage to Madame Lalaurie, mainly to ask that some of his possessions be sent to him (translated by Larry Frank, Delassus–St. Vrain Collection, MHS):

Havana 9 Oct. 1842
Mr. Auguste Delassus, New Orleans

My Dear Auguste,
Perhaps I trouble you, but I dare believe that you would like to render me the service that I ask of you.

You must have in your hands some works that I cannot bring with me; these are works of medicine (some belonged to my father). I would like you to have them delivered to me and at the same time, another object, that I want to possess very much, and which cannot be of any use to you—two diplomas, one of master mason, the other of [illegible] cross of the Lodge of the Friends of the Bourbons of Villeneuve-sur-Lot that belong to me along with an apron in leather, one in silk, with its cord and a cross. Please wrap them together, seal and deliver them to the captain who will deliver them to me by hand since this cannot pass through customs with the case containing the books. This last [item] you will put on the manifest, by sending me the bill of loading [sic], by mail, so that I can claim it immediately, but of that, if within 48 hours one hasn't made entry into customs, he pays a penalty and double duties.

Give me some news, about your father and your family, above all about your oldest son who is also mine; he will undoubtedly not remember he who marked on the right thigh, a remembrance that he will keep all his life. It is at this price he will conserve it. He will say that it is a sad individual who rendered him into existence (i.e. brought him into this world). I will learn, with much pleasure, that you are happy. If you believe that I can be of some assistance to you here, make use of me in all surety.

My respects to your venerable father, greetings to your Jeanne, caresses to your children, and believe me your all-devoted servant and friend.

Dr. L. Lalaurie
Address Dr. L. Lalaurie
Havana
(no such building)
Also give me news of the good and respectable Mrs. Widow Derbigni [sic], your aunt, to whom I pray you to offer the assurance of my respect. Vale.

Louis' death date has not been verified. The search for death and birth records in Cuba is a hard process if you are not in the country. Searches have to be done church by church, and the researcher needs to be able to narrow the search down in years. This proved impossible for us, and it is hoped that future historians will ascertain Louis Lalaurie's date and place of death. Havana, Cuba, is probably a good place to start, as it was also a common stopping point between France and Louisiana.

In 1850, a passport application appeared verifying that Louis Lalaurie of New Orleans was a citizen of the United States (a handwritten document, signature illegible). It is believed that the passport was issued to Louis and Delphine's son, Jean Louis Lalaurie. Jean Louis was six years old at the time of the fire. Based on letters written by Delphine's family, he was with them in Paris early on. It is believed that Jean Louis returned to New Orleans with his mother in the 1840s.

Letters Jean Louis wrote from France on behalf of his mother show an articulate and respectful boy. It appears that he had hearing problems as a young child. He underwent therapy that apparently worked, because after his twelfth year his hearing issues are not mentioned in letters again.

It appears that Jean Louis moved back and forth between Paris and New Orleans and took over the family matters. Correspondence with his uncle, Delassus, shows a maturing young man eager to make business ventures. An 1850 census has "J Laloire" living in New Orleans. This alternative spelling could be a deliberate attempt to shield his soiled family name. More likely, though, it is a typo or perhaps a different family altogether.

Throughout the 1850s, Jean Louis corresponded with Delassus about business, bills and matters pertaining to the family. A large amount of the correspondence is dedicated to business transactions that Jean Louis undertook with Delassus and the Denis family. He certainly did not seem to be hiding from his family name. Whether he faced any repercussions from his mother and stepfather's infamous reputation is completely unknown. He remained unmarried throughout his life.

In 1870, an article in the *New Orleans Times* tells of a duel between Jean Louis Lalaurie and his cousin, Lucien Debuys. Jean Louis was wounded, and rumors circulated that he was bleeding to death. The rumors were untrue; he recovered from his wound. His death is recorded in the New Orleans, Louisiana Death Record Index as December 13, 1883, at the age of fifty-five.

A Marie Lalaurie, two years old, has a death records index entry in 1872. This particular record does not state who her parents were, but no other Lalauries show up in the records. Further research may indicate that this was Jean Louis' illegitimate daughter—and Madame Lalaurie's granddaughter.

Chapter 5
Exiled in Paris

As his only reply, the doctor pointed to the place of Madame de Larcy, (as Lalaurie
was called in this story), which was empty. At that moment, the sound of a carriage
was heard: everyone hurried to the window…a caleche, driven by a negro, appeared and
passed rapidly under the balcony. Madame de Larcy was seated there, calm and proud,
holding in her hand a bouquet of heliotrope.

—L. Souvestre, 1838

After her flight from New Orleans, Madame Lalaurie set up residence in Paris. It is assumed that she stayed at one of the family homes of the Macartys or possibly at the Pontalba residence (the Tallyrand building), which was once used as the French Consulate in Paris. She had her six-year-old son by Louis Lalaurie, Jean Louis, with her. She also had three of her adult children by Jean Blanque: her daughters Pauline and Laure and her son Paulin.

What could have been an early report of Madame Lalaurie appeared in *Le Courier des Estates-Unis* on December 8, 1838. Written by L. Souvestre, who cannot be identified, the piece related the story as told by a Methodist minister, Dr. Miller. In this narrative, Dr. Miller is a guest at the French estate of Henri Vrain. (The Vrains were relatives of the Delassus family.) Dr. Miller recognizes a fellow guest, known to the others as Madame de Larcy, as the notorious Madame Lalaurie. After searching his troubled soul, he tells the other guests of her gruesome actions. Madame Lalaurie flees from the estate at the end of the tale and into obscurity once again.

The Pontalba estate, probable residence of the Lalaurie family during their exile to France. *Library of Congress, Prints and Photographs Division.*

This narrative is melodramatic and reads more like a piece of short fiction than an account of an actual event. However, it is an interesting representation of what Madame might have faced in the tight communities of the French and French Creoles. (See more on the L. Souvestre story in the seventh chapter.)

More probable, though, is that Madame was not hiding at all. She could not be prosecuted in France for what she had allegedly done in New Orleans. Her whereabouts were no secret. Jeanne (Delphine's daughter by Jean Blanque) visited her mother in Paris in the late 1830s with her children and husband, Auguste Delassus, as shown by the numerous pieces of correspondence found in the Missouri History Archives. (Auguste Delassus wrote to his father about a deplorable trip they took to stay with the Lalauries at their estate in Aquitaine. Whether this is the same trip that spurred Delphine's son Paulin to dub the Lalaurie family "jackasses" is unclear.)

Madame Lalaurie gave power of attorney to Jeanne's husband, Auguste Delassus, before she fled New Orleans. Eventually, Jeanne and Delassus separated. Auguste was settling the town of Delassus, Missouri, during the last years of Delphine's life. There is correspondence between Delassus and Delphine regarding her financial welfare and her mental health. (One can only speculate about the inner demons that may have tormented Delphine. Did she feel guilt for her role in the atrocities of 1834? Was she suffering

Located in Aquitaine, France, the Lalaurie estate is now a bed-and-breakfast. Louis Lalaurie's family chateau is the site of Madame's humiliating visit as told by her son-in-law, Auguste Delassus. *Lalaurie estate.*

residual anxiety from her abusive marriage to Louis Lalaurie? Or was her complex psyche simply crumbling under the stress of her exile?) Reading Delphine's correspondence with Delassus leads one to believe that she did not suffer from guilt. Any angst in the subtext of the letters is well hidden.

Jeanne accompanied her mother back to New Orleans about 1842. Laure, Paulin and Pauline resided with Delphine in Paris as late as 1838; they probably fled New Orleans with her after the fire. But Laure maintained her New Orleans residence while she was in France and, by 1842, was back in New Orleans. Receipts show that she was living in the Vieux Carré.

Directories indicate that two of Madame Lalaurie's unmarried daughters, Jeanne and Pauline, returned to New Orleans to live next door to their mother in the mid-1840s. Her son, Paulin, returned to New Orleans and married Felicite Amanda Andry between 1851 and 1853. He fathered two children and died on September 22, 1868.

Madame Lalaurie's eldest daughter, Borquita, lived in New Orleans her entire life, and there is no evidence that she visited her mother during her exile.

Madame Lalaurie thrived in Paris; she seemed to be able to thrive anywhere. She conducted business from France, paying her taxes and financing the repair of a residence in New Orleans (Faubourg Marigny) that was rented out. Records indicate that Madame returned to New Orleans and lived in this house until her death in 1857 or 1858. (See the sixth chapter.)

As for Madame's younger son, he starts to speak for himself as early as age twelve. Louis Lalaurie wrote to his uncle about joining his mother in the country after he had a surgery to improve his hearing. This indicates that Madame was living a life similar to her New Orleans existence—a residence in town, as well as a rural retreat. It would seem that Delphine had a busy social life and not many financial worries at this point in time.

From about 1840 on, however, a different tone appears in Delphine Lalaurie's correspondence to her son-in-law, Auguste Delassus. In a letter from the Delassus–St. Vrain Collection, she inquires repeatedly about her money and Auguste's lack of response to her letters and expresses her angst over the situation:

31 May 1842 ALS
Lalaurie nee Macarty to Auguste Delassus

My Dear Delassus,
I don't know what to attribute the delay to that you have caused in sending me the draft that you are announcing to me in the letter that you wrote to me via Doctor Thomas. What I can tell you is that I have found myself in a painful and most embarrassing position seeing that since the month of last June, I haven't drawn on you. After having waited in vain for the various steamships, which have arrived for some time, that I would receive some news of my affairs, I have been obliged to put my signature out, still hoping that in the interval that would lapse until the due date of the promissory note, I would be able to receive some money; but what was my disappointment and my fears when I saw that my signature could be protested, for they could have been able to refuse to renew my promissory note. It was therefore necessary for me to take some money at an exorbitant premium: I paid 4,80 [piastres]: you see what an enormous loss I take. It is Mr. Artigue, son-in-law of Mr. Shiff, who will draw on you. The drafts will leave on the June 4 boat.
I don't know what to think about your silence toward me since my brother receives letters from you very often. You have announced the state of my affairs to me several times and since the departure of Placide for France, the time at which you were put in charge of them, I still have not been able to receive news of them. I earnestly pray you make the news arrive to me as

soon as you receive this letter, and if the drafts that you were announcing to me haven't left, to send me in place of the first sum asked for, fifteen hundred piastres to complete the five thousand piastres, which I need for my expenses for the year. If the management of my affairs was distracting you from your other occupations, you could ask Placide to take charge of them. I hope that he will not refuse to do so.

Tell Jeanne that I received her letter of 18 April, which gave me so much pleasure since it had been a long time that we were without news, and that which she gave me was good. I was very happy the children were over the measles and that you were all in good health at that time. Nevertheless, Delphine's [Borquita's] little Octave was still convalescing. I hope that he recovered completely soon after Jeanne Wrote me. Please witness to Delphine my satisfaction to have learned of her happy deliver, but tell her at the same time, that I was not so satisfied when I learned she was still pregnant. Nonetheless, I don't love her dear little daughter less, whom I would like to be able, with all the others, to kiss and press to my heart.

We have learned indirectly of the nominations of Placide as comptroller of the banks. They told us that it was worth four thousand piastres a year for him. Since this piece of news was announced to us by two people who learned of it by letters that they had received, we do not in delivering satisfaction that it must naturally inspire us with to expose us to disappointment to which one can often await in adding faith to the news which is distributed here. In the position of Placide, nine children, Jeanne and himself to support, I consider that a position [paying] four thousands piastres would be a great help to him. May the circumstances become favorable to him and may they repair, a little the losses that he has had.

The news of the reunion of your father and the rest of you made me feel a great pleasure. His separation from his sister must have cost him a lot, but the circumstance that brought it will have without a doubt rendered it less painful by thinking that the company of his grandchildren would procure him a little more distraction. The presence of young people in a house always fills it with more gaiety and liveliness.

Kiss your father for me. Give my greetings to your aunt. I reunite you all in my heart to love you and kiss you for me, Pauline and Louis [child].

Delphine's son Paulin wrote to his brother-in-law, Auguste Delassus, that his mother seemed to be using the dire straits of her finances in Louisiana as a catalyst to return to New Orleans. Her children were appalled to even contemplate such an action. But as always, Delphine would do as she pleased.

Chapter 6
Delphine Lalaurie's Last Years

In [January 28,] *1941 a one-time sexton of St. Louis cemeteries said he had discovered a copper plate relating in French that Delphine MacCarthy Lalauire [sic] had died in Paris in 1842 and that her remains were in St. Louis Cemetery No. 1. Descendents at that time said they had long known of this and had visited her tomb.*
—Times-Picayune, *August 9, 1964*

There are several accounts of Delphine's death that have been entertained by storytellers and historians. One report suggests that she was killed by a wild boar in a hunting accident in France, while another, a story that ran in the *Daily Picayune* in March 1892, insists that she died among friends and family in Paris. Still other accounts note that Delphine Lalaurie never left Louisiana and instead dwelled on the north shore of Lake Pontchartrain for the remainder of her days. Current research indicates that all these accounts are wrong—Madame returned to Faubourg Marigny in New Orleans, probably in October 1842, and lived there until her death in the mid- to late 1850s.

Paulin, her son by Jean Blanque, wrote to Auguste Delassus several times, including a very telling letter advising Auguste and his family that Madame Lalaurie was set on returning to New Orleans despite their protestations. Following is a translation by Larry Frank of the Missouri Historical Society (Delassus–St. Vrain Collection). Note the apparent strength of Paulin's feelings and his reference to the events of 1834:

New Orleans' Most Famous Murderess Revealed

Paris 15 August 1842

I just learned that in a letter that my mother wrote to you this morning, she announces to you her arrival at New Orleans for the end of the month of October or the beginning of November. This news undoubtedly will surprise you as it has those to whom my mother has spoken of her return to Louisiana. She has been thinking about this for a long time, but not knowing what pretext to use in order to realize a project of which the idea alone is a lack of consideration toward her family. She has been speaking about it in a vague manner but we comfort ourselves with the hope that moments of humor alone could make her nourish a thought that the sad memories of the catastrophe of 1834 must have made her envision as impossible rolling [sic] *to the feet and the regards due to the family and public opinion, she wants to find a plausible pretext for the general bankruptcy which reigns in Louisiana, in order to leave Paris and realize a dream* [that she has had] *for more than five years. Everywhere she goes, she announces her departments and give as a reason the bad state in which her affairs are found. No, this pretext could be valuable in the eyes of those who do not know my mother, but I, who for four years, have lived with her and who have studied her, I have unfortunately seen that time hasn't changed anything in that indomitable nature and that by her character she was again preparing many sufferings and discomforts for her children. I bemoan (as we must all bemoan) the fate that awaits us if ever my mother puts her feet in that country, or by a generally disapproved of conduct. She has caused us to shed many tears and where she would go we prepare ourselves for news* [due to] *her presence. I truly believe that my mother never had a true idea concerning what the cause of her departure from New Orleans was since she is thinking of returning to that country gain…See Placide when you receive the letter from mother, which announces to you her arrival there; deliberate together and don't let the fear of displeasing her cause you to recoil from what you will have to say to her on the impossibility of her returning to New Orleans. I know that the truth is sometimes painful to speak, but when it can prevent great evils, it is a duty to divulge it and renouncing to do it is a mistake. For me, when I know that her trip has been completely decided upon, then I will fulfill my task here and if my observations result in nothing, the truth, as painful as it is for a son towards a mother from her insane project, then will tell her that Pauline and I won't go with her, and I would also know how to make her see that her project of living with one of her married daughters is impossible because they would never consent to it. My task will be painful, but I have decided to complete it so that later there will be nothing to reproach me for.*

Receipt for work done at Madame Lalaurie's home in the Faubourg Marigny in 1840.

Bills of receipt and other notes from Madame Lalaurie to her son-in-law indicate that she was having a residence she owned in Faubourg Marigny, just off the Vieux Carré in New Orleans, renovated. A receipt dated 1841 shows her paying bills for a property at the corner of Rue Victoire (now Decatur) and Rue Marigny—a mere six blocks from the scene of "the catastrophe of 1834." In the same collection at the Missouri Historical Society Archives are tax bills showing that Delphine and her brother, Barthélémy, owned seven pieces of property worth approximately $138,000, a fortune at this time. City directories confirm that Delphine and her daughters lived in adjacent houses. Unfortunately, the corner Madame lived on is now an industrial section from the turn of the twentieth century, obliterating yet another of the Macarty/Lalaurie historic properties.

Until recently, most historians concurred that Delphine Lalaurie died in France on December 7, 1842, and that her body was secretly returned to New Orleans. This belief was based on a single discovery made in the early 1900s.

Eugene Backes, who served as sexton to St. Louis Cemetery No. 1 until 1924, discovered an old, cracked copper plate in Alley No. 1 of the old graveyard. The inscription on the plate read: "Madame Lalaurie, nee Marie Delphine Maccarthy, decedee a Paris, le' 7 décembre, 1842, a l'age de 6—."

The *Times-Picayune* ran an article recounting the discovery of the Lalaurie plaque.

The *Picayne* ran this article on August 9, 1964, upon the discovery of the plaque, with a picture of Sexton Backes holding the plaque:

> *In 1941 a one-time sexton of St. Louis cemeteries said he had discovered a copper plate relating in French that Delphine MacCarthy Lalauire [sic] had died in Paris in 1842 and that her remains were in St. Louis Cemetery No. 1. Descendents at that time said they had long known of this and had visited her tomb.*

As compelling as the plaque seems to be, it is a clever hoax. Was it a coincidence that the "death date" on the plaque coincided with her actual return to New Orleans? Was the plaque a cruel joke, or was it a ruse to convince the residents of New Orleans that Madame Lalaurie was dead? Regardless of the reasons for the plaque, it was no more than a sham. One credible documented story has someone by the name of N.L. Lalaurie and two of her daughters (Jeanne and Pauline) living in New Orleans until Delphine's death in the mid- to late 1850s—years after the date on the plaque.

In 1850, when Delphine's brother L.B. Macarty's estate was settled, his will directed that property that he had given in his lifetime to his daughter, Maria Louise Macarty, be counted as part of her one-fourth share of the estate. It's possible, even probable, that one-fourth is the "forced share" that children were entitled to receive from their parents' estate no matter what the will said, according to inheritance laws at the time. By designating the previously donated property as Maria's share and leaving her nothing of his current estate, L.B. was essentially, and cleverly, cutting his own daughter out of his will in favor of Delphine.

L.B. Macarty's executors appraised the property left to Maria at $28,100 and took a commission from that. Delphine, Macarty's sole heir under the will, challenged the executors in the Louisiana Supreme Court, arguing (successfully) that the property left to her was never part of the estate and thus they should not have gotten a commission on it. So not only did Delphine get her brother's whole estate, but she also neatly cut the executors out of their commission. This shows that Madame was not only alive but also had the facilities to do some fancy legal wrangling, according to the May 13, 1850 *Times-Picayune*.

To further support the idea of a death date much later than 1842, an advertisement appeared in 1858 in the *New Orleans Times* for the sale of "parcels" to settle Madame Lalaurie's estate. However, no burial notice for Delphine Lalaurie appeared in New Orleans newspapers at that time—or at any other time. It's possible that it took sixteen years to settle her estate, but even considering Madame Lalaurie's financial nagging of Auguste Delassus, it seems unlikely to have taken so long. We have concluded that Delphine Lalaurie died in New Orleans between 1855 and 1858.

So where is Madame Lalaurie buried? Jean Blanque, the Blanque daughters and Madame Lalaurie all rest in unknown burial sites. Because Madame's first child, Borquita, married into the Forstall family, it stands to reason that they are buried in the Forstall burial plot, either in St. Louis Cemetery No. 1 or No. 2. (The Forstalls have large family plots in both cemeteries.)

The Historic Preservation Program (Graduate School of Fine Arts at the University of Pennsylvania) conducted an extensive survey of all of the tombs in St. Louis Cemetery No. 1. Tomb no. 323 is allotted to the extended Forstall family, with interments dating from 1823 until 1850.

To further complicate the mystery of where Madame Lalaurie is buried, there is a burial record for a Delphine López in the St. Louis Cemetery No.

Right: The Forstall family tomb in New Orleans St. Louis Cemetery—perhaps the final resting place of Madame Lalaurie. *Photo by Victoria Cosner Love.*

Below: New Orleans St. Louis Cemetery No. 1, Alley No. 4. The location of the false burial plaque is found here. *Photo by Victoria Cosner Love.*

2 crypt of the Forstall plots. It is thought that the record refers to Borquita, but it is possible that Madame Lalaurie was buried under another name to protect her body from exhumation or desecration.

Still another theory is that she is buried in the Delassus family plots. And, of course, the Macarty tombs have to be considered, even though most of the Macartys were older or deceased by the time Madame Lalaurie died.

Finally, one needs to remember that in New Orleans bodies often stay in the burial chamber only until they decompose. They are then removed to make room for more interments. Delphine Lalaurie's bones are, by now, quite possibly mixed with dozens of others in an anonymous crypt.

Perhaps it is best that Madame Lalaurie's final resting place remains unknown, for the sake of her descendants and the families of those who may be buried with her.

Chapter 7
Madame Lalaurie in Popular History and Culture

After I painted the first, I became fascinated with her innocence. So I did a few more; I guess I was trying to see who was this face so evil, who had done all she was so rightfully accused of.
—Ricardo Pustanio, painter of the famous Haunted House *Delphine Lalaurie portrait*

As the truth is slowly uncovered, it will be interesting to look at how the story has been viewed and reported since the night of the incident. The *Bee* articles are available online and in this book, but there is a lot more material we have not yet revealed. By following these narratives, one can see Madame Lalaurie growing in myth and legend.

L. SOUVESTRE

As we mentioned in the fifth chapter, an article published in *Le Courrier Etats-Unis* on December 8, 1838 (found at Northwestern State University of Louisiana), written by L. Souvestre, tells of what seems to be an eyewitness report of the events in the Lalaurie Mansion by a Methodist minister identified as "Dr. Miller." This article places Madame Lalaurie (known in this story as Madame de Larcy) at the estate of Henri Vrain, her in-law through Delassus, in the Paris suburbs of Saint-Cloud, France, not long after the fire. The fact that these relatives weren't commonly known by most storytellers gives the story a boost of credence.

However, the structure and the writing style are more indicative of a short story, and no "Dr. Miller" can be identified as an actual historical character.

This article or short story seems to reinforce (or perhaps invent) some of the more popular details that turn up in New Orleans ghost tours: the "coachman who glowed with health," the story of Madame passing her glass of wine to a slave and the emaciated, fearful slaves who initially made people wonder what was going on in the mansion.

In addition, this story gives a solid reason for a slave to start the fire, as it was her child who fell to his (or her, as more commonly told) death while being chased by Madame.

There are many differences between this story and popular legends. "Dr. Miller's" account has a young boy, Mingo, as the child who was chased off the roof in 1833 instead of a young girl who pulled a tangle in her mistress's hair and incurred Madame's wrath. He also cites Madame Lalaurie as thrice a widow when these events happened. Louis Lalaurie was not dead in 1834, and multiple eyewitnesses place him at the scene of the fire, annoying his neighbors. Madame is described as young when she would have been at least fifty in 1834. Her daughters are described as children. They were, in fact, young women in 1834. Her young son by Louis Lalaurie was the only child in the house.

Whether this melodramatic piece is fiction (which the authors are inclined to believe) or an embellished version of the truth, it shows that the Lalaurie tale was not only alive and well in 1838 but also that, four years after the incident, it was already changing shape. (Read the entire L. Souvestre story at www.mad-madame-lalaurie.com.)

Harriet Martineau

The first written non-eyewitness account of the story is attributed to Harriet Martineau (1802–1876), a British author, abolitionist and philosopher. During her lifetime, she was recognized as a controversial journalist, political economist, travel writer and feminist. Her *Retrospect of Western Travel* in three volumes chronicles her visit to the United States in 1838–40. She traveled extensively, visiting almost every region of what was the United States at that time.

Her storytelling was brilliant. She vividly evoked many scenes of American life for her British audience. However, she often seemed to base her observations on what she was seeing at the moment; for example, she described New Hampshire as dark and desolate, but she was there during winter. She reported what was told to her by locals with no research into the actual events and as seen through the thick lenses of an abolitionist and feminist.

Interestingly enough, her account of Madame Lalaurie is seen only through the eyes of the abolitionist. No consideration of Madame Lalaurie as a woman in Creole society is given. That being said, her version of the story is quoted or repeated in almost every piece that covers the Lalaurie story.

Martineau began her account by describing the beautiful setting of the road along Lake Pontchartrain and then segued into the following: "It was along this road that Madame Lalaurie escaped from the hands of her exasperated countrymen, about five years ago." A fine way to start a tale of gothic horror, even one that happens to be true.

One of the initial mysteries, that of why Dr. Lalaurie is minimized in folklore and is seldom mentioned as a co-perpetrator of the torture, originated in Martineau's narrative: "Her third husband, M. Lalaurie, was I believe, a Frenchman. He was many years younger than his lady, and had nothing to do with the management of her property; so that he has been in no degree mixed up with her affairs and disgraces."

Whether or not that was true, Ms. Martineau's compelling account made sure that the image of Dr. Lalaurie as a passive background figure became stuck in popular folklore.

The lawyer who was allegedly concerned about the rumors of maltreatment of the Lalaurie slaves was a friend of Ms. Martineau's. Because he was American, and thus not an insider in Creole society, he sent his young Creole student to the Lalaurie house to inform the Lalauries of the Code Noir restrictions. The clerk supposedly returned to his employer starry-eyed and utterly charmed by Madame. This part of the Lalaurie story is told in most every version, oral and written. The identity of the lawyer is never revealed. Martineau referred to him only as "a friend of mine, an eminent lawyer."

Her next bit of narration told of the young slave girl, about eight years old according to Martineau, who was chased onto the roof by Madame and fell to her death in the courtyard. She told this as a secondhand account from a witness whose property adjoined the Lalaurie house. Martineau alleged that the little body was carried off by grieving slaves and then buried in the courtyard where she died. Martineau went on to say that an inquiry was opened to investigate the death and that Madame was found guilty of cruelty. The judge ordered that nine slaves, "who were forfeited according to law," be removed from the Lalaurie house. She claimed that the Madame used family connections to purchase these same slaves back for the sole reason of imprisoning and torturing them, "for she could not let them be seen in a neighborhood where they were known."

It is assumed by many storytellers and writers that the seven slaves who were pulled from the fire were these very slaves. Although this is an enduring part of the legend, its veracity is somewhat dubious. The entire story was told secondhand and even thirdhand to Harriet Martineau. Our later investigation revealed that no court records exist for the death of the slave child nor of any legal judgment against Madame.

One tidbit of gossip that Martineau included, which is not commonly included in the lore, is that Delphine was an abusive mother:

> *It appears that she beat her daughters as often as they attempted in her absence to convey food to her miserable victims. She always knew of such attempts by means of the sleek coachman, who was her spy. It was necessary to have a spy, to preserve her life from the vengeance of her household: so she pampered this obsequious negro, and at length owed her escape to him.*

Interestingly, author Barbara Hambly described Madame's daughters as abused in her excellent novel *Fever Season*, although the abuse seems to be more mental than physical.

We doubt the factuality of the physical abuse, at least. Delphine Lalaurie's daughters remained faithful to her throughout their lives, often traveling and living with her. Letters between Madame and her girls indicate a warm relationship. (As an aside, it is not uncommon for psychopathic or sociopathic individuals to love their own family members, as much as they are capable. Many spouses and relatives of psychopaths are utterly surprised that their loved one could have ever done such bad things—they never saw that aspect of the perpetrator's personality.) Martineau's description of the fire differed from most retellings. She stated that it was extinguished fairly quickly and that the neighbors took advantage of this to break into the "outhouse" (outbuilding) to satisfy their curiosity about the rumors of cruelty.

She painted the Lalauries' escape as being Bastien's idea, as his mistress was so self-absorbed that she had no idea that a bloodthirsty mob was ready to tear her apart. The description of her escape is exciting and dramatic. Martineau's description of the mob reaching the lake too late to catch Madame and instead taking their vengeance out on the horses and, most probably, Bastien is frequently quoted (though unverified).

Martineau related that Madame Lalaurie escaped the howling mob and fled to France but did not stay in one place for long before she was recognized and had to run again. Madame, she believed, "is supposed to be now skulking about in some French province, under a false name."

This rumor of disgrace and exile is found throughout the later legends but is probably not true. Madame would not have had much reason to hide her identity in France, where she could not even be charged with a crime.

Martineau ended her account with a paragraph about the mob setting off to find other cruel masters and distributing circulars. Martineau could "never get out of the way of the horrors of slavery in this region." That may or may not have been true. There are no newspaper accounts of mobs randomly searching Creole homes for cruel masters. It seems doubtful that such a thing would have been permitted by the New Orleans police, who were almost entirely French Creole at the time.

Martineau's tale set the standard for the vilification of Madame Lalaurie. She set Dr. Lalaurie aside as ineffectual, setting the blame squarely on the shoulders of Delphine. Her dramatic descriptions, which she says she collected from eyewitnesses, defamed Madame Lalaurie forever. Martineau gave us a spectacular narrative from just five years after the events, but most of what she reported is hearsay. As for the veracity of eyewitnesses, just speak with any law enforcement officer. Eyewitnesses are considered by many in police work to be the least reliable source of evidence. The brain plays tricks on us. We see what we expect to see, and what we hear about an event can color our memories of it later. Fortunately or unfortunately, Martineau helped set the stage for the story to grow from a shameful case of cruel abuse to an epic Grand Guignol horror show.

HENRY C. CASTELLANOS

Historian Castellanos wrote a history called *New Orleans As It Was: Episodes of Louisiana Life*, which dedicates a chapter to the Lalaurie story. He took some time to research and analyze the story, probably for the first time since the events occurred. He was a contemporary of George Washington Cable's, publishing in the late 1890s. Castellanos added some historical documentation to the tale:

> *The proprietor of the New Orleans "Bee" wrote: "We saw where the collar and manacles had cut their way into their quivering flesh. For several months they had been confined in those dismal dungeons, with no other nutriment than a handful of gruel and an insufficient quantity of water, suffering the tortures*

of the damned and longingly awaiting death, as a relief to their sufferings. We saw Judge Canonge, Mr. Montreuil and others, making for some time fruitless efforts to rescue those poor unfortunates, whom the infamous woman, Lalaurie, had doomed to certain death and hoping that the devouring element might thus obliterate the last traces of her nefarious deeds."

He also corrected what he believed to be erroneous information in previous accounts and backed up his research when he could. For example, a rumor had been going around that many of the rescued slaves died after being fed because they were just too weak to handle nutrition after months of starvation. Castellanos refuted this:

Two thousand persons, at least, convinced themselves during that eventful day by ocular inspection of the martyrdom to which those poor, degraded people had been subjected, while the ravenous appetite with which they devoured the food placed before them fully attest their sufferings from hunger. None of them, however, died from surfeit, as it has been erroneously alleged. Numberless instruments of torture, not the least noticeable of which were iron collars, "carcaus" with sharp cutting edges were spread out upon a long deal table, as evidences of guilt.

He agreed with Martineau on several points, though, including the idea that the fire was purposely set by a slave: "Among them, a woman confessed to the Mayor that she had purposely set fire to the house as the only means of putting an end to her sufferings."

Many tellers of this tale do not look at the activities of the police during the three days after the fire. Some say that all the manpower in New Orleans was needed to protect the Lalaurie house from being reignited and burned to the ground. No account has been found that tells if there was an active effort by law enforcement to capture Madame and Dr. Lalaurie as they fled. Castellanos shined a small light onto what the city authorities were considering:

It was said that Etinue Mazureau, the Attorney General, had expressed his determination to wreak upon the guilty parties the extreme vengeance of the law. But when the shadows of night fell upon the city, and it was ascertained beyond a doubt that no steps in that direction had been taken and that powerful influences were at work to shield the culprits, their fury then knew no bounds and assumed at once an active form.

One item that Castellanos cleared up is whether the bones of the murdered slave girl (and perhaps other victims) were found in the courtyard:

> *The story that human bones and among others those of a child who had committed self-destruction to escape the merciless lash, had been found in a well, is not correct, for the papers of the day report that acting under that belief, the mob had made diligent search even to the extent of excavating the whole yard, and had found nothing.*

Henry Castellanos is a must-read for the Lalaurie enthusiast. He closed his chapter with his belief about the state of the house, as it stood at the time of his writing:

> *As a school house; as a private residence, as a factor; as a commercial house and place of traffic, all of these have been tried, but every venture has proved a ruinous failure. A year or two ago, it was the receptacle of the scum of Sicilian immigrants, and the fumes of the malodorous filth which emanated from its interior proclaimed it what it really is, "A HOUSE ACCURSED."*

This highly entertaining (if extremely racist) ending to the account makes a dramatic denouement to Castellanos's story. However, it is a little surprising that a writer who was so careful with his research into the facts would end on a superstitious note. This just proves that the Lalaurie story affects all who hear it—not just intellectually but at the gut level, the fearful, irrational level where monsters are real and ghosts haunt the house of pain.

GEORGE WASHINGTON CABLE

The American novelist George Washington Cable was probably the most famous writer to spread the Lalaurie legend. Born in Louisiana in 1844, Cable fought for the Confederate army and later became a journalist. His stories of Creole life, before and after the Civil War, painted an incredible picture of pride, opulence, racism and money. His eye for detailing the "battle" between the Americans and French Creole was remarkable, especially in his novel *The Grandissimes*. He conveyed a sense of disapproval toward the racism still present in Louisiana after the War Between the States. Cable eventually moved to Massachusetts and became friends with Mark Twain. They toured together doing book lectures.

George Washington Cable shared tales of Creole culture and its secrets and mysteries with a large American audience. *Library of Congress, Prints and Photographs Division.*

In his book *Strange True Stories of Louisiana*, Cable was one of the first to relate the story of the haunting of the Lalaurie house. He described the basics of the story, mostly sticking to the facts. (It is notable that he did not include any "medical experiment" injuries in the list of tortures suffered by the slaves.) He claimed that Judge Canongo took leadership to look for the household slaves in the garret rooms. He cited neighbors Montreuil, Fernandez and Lefebrve as assisting in the rescue. These accounts are backed up with original documents and depositions given after the incident in 1834.

Initially, rival Louisiana historian Charles Gayerré referred to Cable as "no more than a malevolent, ignorant dwarf," but Cable's popularity and fame as a Creole historian climbed. Gayerré, who was a notorious Creole loyalist in his views of Louisiana history, joined with other New Orleans elite families and led a campaign to defame Cable. Included in his attacks were "sizzling editorials" in the *New Orleans Bee* and a spurious story that Madame Lalaurie had refused to receive Cable in her house because he had "colored blood." Gayerré claimed that Cable wrote his story of the "Haunted House in Royal Street" to get even for this slight. The story is laughable, considering that Cable was born in 1844—a full ten years after Madame and Dr. Lalaurie fled

New Orleans, making him about thirteen years old when Madame Lalaurie died, according to historian Christopher Benfey.

As Cable's popularity grew with American audiences, his fate was sealed among the Creole families in New Orleans. Benfey quotes Louisiana historian Grace King, who wrote that "Cable proclaimed his preference for colored people over white and assumed the inevitable superiority—according to his theories—of the quadroons over the Creoles."

Obviously, this caused him to be persona non grata among the Creole elite. To his credit, Cable didn't seem to care.

Cable published and traveled, and he never backed down from his revelations about the inner workings of Creole society. This earned him the title of "the most cordially hated little man in New Orleans," at least according to New Orleans author Joseph Pennell, quoted by Benfey.

GHOST STORIES ABOUND

The ghost stories surrounding the Lalaurie incident are perhaps the pieces of the story that are the most repeated, most widely spread and most creatively embellished. You won't find a haunted New Orleans tour that doesn't include ghosts along with the grisly details of torture and mayhem. If you ask any longtime citizen where to find the most haunted house in New Orleans, they'll direct you to the house on Royal Street.

JEANNE DELAVIGNE

Enter Jeanne DeLavigne, who wrote *Ghost Stories of Old New Orleans* in 1946. It not only set the standard for tales of hauntings in the Lalaurie house, but it was also quite possibly responsible for some of the gorier embellishments on what the rescuers found during the Lalaurie house fire of 1834, including the medical experiments and buckets of body parts. There is no documentation to back up these aspects of the story. DeLavigne wrote a horror story, not a history:

> *The man who smashed the garret door saw powerful male slaves, stark naked, chained to the wall, their eyes gouged out, their fingernails pulled off by the roots; others had their joints skinned and festering, great holes in their buttocks where the flesh had been sliced away, their ears hanging by shreds,*

Image from the DeLavigne book of a torture victim hanging upside down.

their lips sewed together, their tongues drawn out and sewed to their chins, severed hands stitched to bellies, legs pulled joint from joint. Female slaves there were, their mouths and ears crammed with ashes and chicken offal and bound tightly; others had been smeared with honey and were a mass of black ants. Intestines were pulled out and knotted around naked waists. There were holes in skulls, where a rough stick had been inserted to stir the brains. Some of the poor creatures were dead, some were unconscious; and a few were still breathing, suffering agonies beyond any power to describe.
[DeLavigne quoted the firemen entering the house.]

This book, sadly out of print, is a classic of New Orleans ghost story literature. If you find a copy, consider yourself very lucky.

Interestingly enough, firsthand stories of hauntings in the Lalaurie house have appeared in newspapers and periodicals over the years, particularly at Halloween. This *States Item* report from June 16, 1969, notes an appearance:

Zella Funck lives in the famous "Haunted House" at 1140 Royal St. "My poltergeists are just playful," she declares blithely. "They're not around every day, but they do surprise visitors."...The ghost, whom she says she has seen twice, is a romantic figure of a man. "I've watched him for several minutes in a full-length mirror before he faded away. He's about 5'9", about 170 lbs, has a reddish clipped beard, and wears a creamy beige felt hat turned up slightly, with a cord around it."

This *Times-Picayune* item from August 11, 1974, reports another:

As recently as 14 years ago, a long-time resident of one of the small apartments within the building declared emphatically that he had heard strange sounds near his room for as long as he had lived there—footsteps running along dim passages, mournful sighs and, at least once, a smothered scream. He didn't bother to investigate, he said, and so the spirits—or whatever they were—hadn't bothered him.

Of course, if you search for "Lalaurie ghost stories" on the Internet, you will find a veritable treasure-trove of material. Like most Internet content, it is to be taken with a huge grain of salt. But searching for Madame on the web from time to time is an entertaining way of finding out how the legends have most recently been adapted.

CREATING THE FACE OF A MONSTER

There are two images of Madame Lalaurie that float through the Internet. One is a realistic-looking painting depicting Delphine in an 1880s-style dress. The other painting is more eerie, painted in unsettling reds and blacks. Both paintings were created by the same New Orleans artist, Ricardo Pustanio.

Pustanio's first portrait of Madame Lalaurie is the most commonly found image of Madame on the Internet. Very similar to a 1934 portrait published in the *Times-Picayune*, the red and black painting of the infamous Madame Delphine Lalaurie was painted in 1997 and has grown its own legend. As spooky as it is, there is nothing strange about its creation or the reasons Pustanio decided to paint it. "At the time I used whatever image of her I could find to do the work from," said Pustanio, both on a website and in his interview with one of the authors. "I even went to the Musée Conti Historical Wax Museum and questioned them about her appearance they did in wax."

With no detailed description of Madame Lalaurie in the chronicles of history (other than the often-repeated comment that she was beautiful), Pustanio and the Musée Conti were on their own in creating her image.

Pustanio told the authors in an interview that he was asked to create this image by a resident of the Lalaurie house. This gentleman wanted to have her portrait in their apartment as a touchstone with the building's past. Besides, they said, it would make a great conversation piece. Pustanio obliged, creating a haunting, unforgettable image. The painting was perhaps more haunting than Pustanio intended, for it gathered its *own* reputation for being haunted.

After they hung it on the wall, the piece took on a life of its own, according to the portrait's owners. "The resident began to hold séances for his friends and even tourists and paranormal investigators, who always are trying to get a glimpse inside the haunted mansion," said Pustanio. "To their astonishment the painting would actually rock on the wall and even fall loose from the wall, hitting the floor with a great thud."

The owner eventually became frightened by the painting. He reported smelling smoke, having objects in his apartment moved around by unseen forces and other strange phenomena. He gave the portrait to one of the other tenants of the mansion. She hung it proudly, but she also started having problems with the painting. She heard pacing footsteps and strange sounds. The portrait's eyes followed her across the room. Cold hands touched her. When she started hearing the painting whisper to her, she brought in a paranormal investigator to document the incidents. (The complete story of the haunted portrait can be read at the Haunted America Tours website.)

Pustanio often heard the story of a haunted painting bandied about, but he did not at first realize that the painting in question was one that he had created. "[N]ever did I think the Haunted Painting was something that I had done," the artist was quoted as saying. "I've done a lot of things in my life that people say are haunted. I personally don't think I am haunted. Nor does what I do attract ghosts, or is intended to be haunted."

"I just think outright some people connect with artists, because we put strong emotions into our works," he continued. "And isn't a haunting basically supposed to be just that, strong emotions of the dead manifesting themselves?"

During his interview with the authors, the artist commented that he was very happy about the portrait being his, even though it did nothing of a supernatural nature when it was returned to him by its second owner. "It is great publicity to paint a haunted portrait," he said.

Pustanio went on to say that he found the portrait a new home and that the new owners will not discuss the portrait. When Pustanio was asked why his portraits of Madame depict her in the wrong period costume, he replied that this detail was requested by the patrons. No one wanted her in the lovely French Empire–style dress that she would have worn to grace the salons of Creole New Orleans. They wanted Victoriana, perhaps because the high collars and dark ruffles are seen as more gothic. He also noted that people always describe Madame Lalaurie to him as a tall woman, and he envisioned her as smaller with dark hair and eyes. Perhaps that was true, or maybe she retained the Irish fairness of her father's side of the family. Pustanio is the only one, besides the Musée Conti Historical Wax Museum, that has so far put a face to this legend.

An interesting aside: during the interview, Pustanio revealed that his interest in the Lalaurie family stems from a personal connection to the story. His family historically owned land around St. John's Bayou, where Delphine was said to have escaped the screaming mob.

Pustanio's family ran a fish business that focused on the Creole elite. Pustanio still graces the Mardi Gras parades with his imaginative floats, winning awards almost every year. He is also available to paint by commission if you want your own portrait of the mad Madame Lalaurie or of her Devil Baby of Bourbon Street.

Musée Conti Historical Wax Museum

The Musée Conti Historical Wax Museum, located at 917 Rue Conti in the Vieux Carré, displays a wax rendition of Madame Lalaurie. When the authors asked around the shops and bars of the French Quarter, people often called the likeness of Madame Lalaurie "obscene." Most people on the street believe that the wax image shows Madame whipping the slave child before the child fell from the roof of the mansion.

In fact, the museum has Madame dressed in a pink and white dress from the 1830s, holding a candle up while her slave, Bastien (we assume), is shown whipping two slaves who are obviously starved and chained in the attic. It has not been changed since the museum opened in the 1970s.

Not a wholesome image, but it is certainly a different tableau than the one at least a dozen people described to the authors. It's fascinating that such tales are being passed around and embellished regarding an in-town display that can be viewed at any time. Perhaps the average citizens of New Orleans have no taste for tourist destinations like the wax museum. Or maybe they're just too tired of the hideous story to want to see it played out in realistic wax figures.

One of the few attempts to put a face to Madame Lalaurie, the Musée Conti Historical Wax Museum in New Orleans shows Madame and her faithful servant beating starved slaves. *Photo by Victoria Cosner Love.*

IN THE MODERN PRESS

In 1934, the *Times-Picayune* published an article on the 100th anniversary of the Lalaurie fire, featuring a portrait of a lovely woman. The articles reported that the woman in the portrait is Delphine Lalaurie. The face looks hauntingly similar to Pustanio's images.

WEBSITES

Dozens of websites are dedicated to Madame Lalaurie. According to the many pages of the World Wide Web, Madame Lalaurie is guilty of serial killings, sending voodoo curses, raising a Devil Baby, turning her slaves into zombies and plenty of other horrid but rather ridiculous and unbelievable crimes. Most websites quote one another or the same *Bee* articles sourced

A Madame Lalaurie portrait
as shown in a 1934 newspaper
article. Could it be?

above, over and over. Many websites relate one variation or another of
the core story, with some embellishment and artistic license. Some seem
to espouse ideas pulled from the webmaster's own head, not based in fact,
rumor or even logic.

You'll find a list at the end of this book of lore-related Lalaurie sites. Don't
visit them for solid information, but definitely visit them. You'll find some
outrageously entertaining material. These sites are a must-see for enthusiasts
of the Lalaurie legend.

BARBARA HAMBLY

In *Fever Season*, a novel of historical fiction, author Barbara Hambly enmeshes
her hero, a free man of color named Ben January, in the Lalaurie story. Her
research into the subject was meticulous. Her portrait of New Orleans in
1834 is amazingly realistic and utterly engrossing.

Hambly takes a definite opinion on Madame Lalaurie, describing her as a sexual sadist almost solely responsible for the atrocities against the slaves. Whether or not that was the case, she portrays Delphine beautifully as a coldhearted, controlling sociopath, which could well have been the truth.

Hambly even notes that Dr. Lalaurie was working on medicine to help correct malformations, as we noted in the fourth chapter. This is a little-known historic tidbit and illustrates the incredible level of research that went into her book. This novel is by far one of the best and most entertaining fictional accounts of the Lalaurie story.

MOVIES

One would think that Hollywood would find the Madame Lalaurie story irresistible. However, we have not been able to find a single historical drama about the incident.

We did find a low-budget horror movie set in contemporary times but based (loosely) around the Lalaurie legend: *The St. Francisville Experiment*, from Trimark Pictures, 2000. The film features four young ghost hunters entering a "haunted house" in St. Francisville, Louisiana, where Madame Lalaurie was said (according to the movie) to have continued her atrocities after fleeing New Orleans in 1834. The film was shot at the lovely Ellerslie Plantation, which is actually located outside of St. Francisville. This film is a *Blair Witch Project*-style faux documentary, shot with handheld video cameras. Although the town of St. Francisville does have a number of ghost stories connected with it, including the famously "haunted" Myrtles plantation house, there are no actual stories connecting it to Madame Lalaurie.

TELEVISION

The Lalaurie house and its supposed hauntings have been mentioned on a number of documentary and reality TV programs. The legend was showcased on the History Channel's *Haunted History* series, and the Lalaurie story comes up often in "Ghost Hunter" and "Most Haunted" TV shows. Watch your TV listings, particularly around Halloween, and you'll most likely find something about the Lalauries.

Chapter 8
What If It's All True?

The slaves were the property of the demon in the shape of a woman whom we mentioned in the beginning of this article. They had been confined by her for several months in the situation from which they had thus been rescued and had merely been kept in existence to prolong their sufferings and to make them taste all that the most refined cruelty could inflict.

—New Orleans Bee, *April 1834*

There is nothing funny about what happened to the unfortunate souls trapped in the garret of the Lalaurie house in 1834. That was a tragic and horrible event. But if one were to look at every aspect of the legend, including the more outlandish parts, it starts to get just a bit ridiculous.

To play devil's advocate, your authors would like to present a worst-case scenario: what if it's all true? Every rumor, every tale and every gory detail? Let's take a look.

In our worst-case alternate reality, Delphine has been wicked since birth. She slyly managed to kill both of her previous husbands in order to inherit their money. She found a soul mate in Louis Lalaurie—they both have a taste for blood.

Delphine and Louis Lalaurie are serial killers. They have been killing slaves for years, from the time they moved into the house on Royal Street. Their reasons for killing are different, but they are equally deadly. When a slave perishes at their hands, he is buried beneath the floorboards of the house or perhaps taken out to the swamp in the dead of night and dumped as food for the alligators. They also keep a number of slaves chained in the

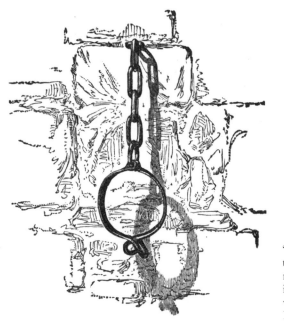

"We only permit masters, when they shall think that the case requires it, to put their slaves in irons, and to have them whipped with rods or ropes." From the Louisiana Code Noir, 1724.

attic at all times so they are available if either Lalaurie suddenly has the impulse to kill or torture.

Madame kills and maims slaves because she is naturally cruel and because she was driven insane by the murder of her parents, who died in a slave uprising. She is now completely mad and a sadist—perhaps even a sexual sadist. She takes perverse pleasure in starving her slaves and watching them waste away before her eyes. She glories in the fact that their lives are entirely in her hands.

She flogs her slaves mercilessly for the slightest mistake. She pours salt water into their wounds, binds their mouths shut and coats them with honey so that ants will devour them. Anything that pops into the fetid jungle that is her mind she is likely to perpetrate on her poor, hapless bondsmen.

Madame puts forth an image of tranquility and social grace. She is beautiful and charming, and her parties are legendary. All of Creole society loves and envies her. Delphine and Louis live in their stylish Creole mansion with two of Delphine's adult daughters from her marriage to the handsome pirate, Jean Blanque, and with her young son with Louis Lalaurie. She takes a perverse pleasure in maintaining a perfect façade, while her private life is a twisted hell of sickness and brutality.

Bastien, Madame Lalaurie's driver, is a willing accomplice in her crimes. He has no compassion for his fellow slaves and will beat them just as readily

New Orleans' Most Famous Murderess Revealed

as Madame will. He is utterly loyal to Delphine—the moment she tells him to do something, he does it. He works as a spy for Madame. If her waiflike daughters try to sneak food to any of the slaves, Bastien tells Madame, who beats the girls without mercy. He lords his power over the slaves as much as any overseer would.

Why is he so loyal to his cruel mistress? Is it simply because she feeds him well, clothes him beautifully and treats him with kindness? Or is it something more? Perhaps he shares her taste for sadism. And perhaps he and Madame are lovers. Once again, Delphine defies society's norms, twisting them to fit her self-centered and perverse inner world.

Louis Lalaurie does not consider himself a sadist. He is a doctor, and he conducts experiments out of scientific curiosity. He started out with good intentions. He drafted the occasional unlucky slave to be a test subject for his work in curing skeletal deformities. But once he realized that he had utter power and control over these people, all self-control fled. He does anything to the bodies of his slaves that enters his imagination. And his imagination is very vivid.

Can a person survive if you drill a hole into his head? What happens if you stir his brain with a stick? How much skin does a person need? How much can you peel away before she dies? Can the human body adapt if you break every large bone and reset them at bizarre angles? Will she still be able to move? If you cut the sexual organs from a person of one sex and sew them onto another, can you change the sex of the subject?

The doctor's experiments are extremely messy. Buckets of body parts litter the attic. He has asked Bastien to dispose of them, but the haughty servant answers only to Madame. No matter. Perhaps the doctor will think of some use for the severed limbs.

In addition to his surgical experiments, Dr. Lalaurie has been experimenting with "zombie powder" in an attempt to create the perfect, utterly obedient slave. He is supplied with the highly toxic ingredients by Marie Laveau, New Orleans' reigning voodoo queen. His subjects are Marie's enemies, as well as his own slaves. Time and time again he has administered the powder to bound and helpless subjects. Unlike his predecessors in Haiti, he has not yet succeeded in creating a docile zombie.

Most of his subjects simply die after suffering extreme pain and paralysis. Some go mad, ranting and raving at invisible tormentors. These subjects Dr. Lalaurie has to kill quickly to prevent them from raising too much ruckus. Some fall into a deep, staring unconsciousness and never awaken. These people are used in Dr. Lalaurie's surgical experiments. Madame Lalaurie is not interested in them. She only likes victims who are able to scream.

The Musée Conti Historical Wax Museum displays a wax presentation of Marie Laveau providing goods for a bride. *Photo by Victoria Cosner Love, permission of Musée Conti Historical Wax Museum.*

In addition to the abattoir in their attic, the Lalauries have other secrets. One of them is the Devil Baby of Bourbon Street, who lives in a small, dark room at the back of the house. This monstrous, deformed child was given to Delphine by Marie Laveau. The voodoo queen claims that the child was cursed, born of a union between a fine Creole lady and a swamp devil. Judging by the unearthly howls and shrieks the little creature emits, the Lalauries suspect that she may be right.

When the baby was baptized, Madame Lalaurie stood as his godmother. She and Marie Laveau each have their own motives for keeping the baby alive. Laveau wants the child for blackmail and to add to her own fearful reputation. Madame just finds him amusing.

A "Devil Baby" skull sculpture. The "Devil Baby" of Bourbon Street has inspired generations of artists and ghost hunters. *Authors' collection.*

Delphine delights in the Devil Baby. She finds his screams and spasms endlessly amusing. She spends hours watching the child, petting him and feeding him bloody bits of raw meat. Louis, too, is fascinated with the baby. He would love to dissect it, but Delphine shoos him away.

Delphine's sanity seems to be slipping further away. She starves even the slaves who serve her in the house. Visitors have begun to whisper about their gaunt, miserable appearance. When no one is visiting, she forces the slaves to go naked or shirtless, simply to humiliate them. Her daughters, always by her side, seem timid, pale and scared. Her temper is as volatile as an angry alligator's. The slightest misstep sends her into a fury. She keeps a bullwhip in her boudoir, and she is an expert with it.

One evening, Nina, a little slave child, accidentally pulls Madame's hair while brushing it. Madame goes mad with fury, chasing the girl to the roof of the house and lashing her with the bullwhip. The terrified Nina, given the choice between the raving Madame and the cobblestoned courtyard below, chooses death. Her little body strikes the stones with a sickening crunch. Madame stares dispassionately down at her for a moment and then goes back inside the house. The servants wait until Madame is abed. Quietly, like shadows, they carry the child's broken body to the kitchen. The women tenderly wash her while the men dig a shallow grave by the well in the courtyard.

Nina's is not the first corpse to be interred there. It is almost certainly not the last. But someone has had enough. Nina's grandmother, Rachael, an old kitchen slave, seethes with fury. She vows revenge against her mistress.

What Delphine does not know is that a horrified neighbor witnessed the chase and the whipping and hid her eyes as little Nina plummeted to her death. The authorities are called in. Delphine is called to court, where she perfectly balances her false grief for the "accidental" death of the child with her well-practiced charm. The judge, a relative of Delphine's, wants to dismiss the case, but the city is simmering with rumors about the incident. He orders Delphine to pay a fine of $300, which she can well afford. He also orders her remaining slaves, with the exception of Bastien and Rachael, to be removed from her property and sold.

Madame does not appreciate the negative press, but it takes much more than that to rattle her. She quickly and quietly arranges for another relative to buy the slaves back for her.

She blames the slaves for her public embarrassment. Thick, heavy, spiked chains are attached to their necks, wrists and legs, and they are locked in the attic to await her "attention." If her treatment of them was bad before, it now escalates to horrifying proportions.

Delphine is particularly irritated with Rachael, the grandmother of the dead slave child Nina. Rachael has always been a magnificent cook, making Delphine's friends jealous with the culinary treats that roll from her kitchen. But now Rachael grows defiant, refusing to cook. One minute Rachael can be found mourning pitiably for her lost grandchild and the next raging for vengeance. Madame, unconcerned as usual, chains her to the big kitchen stove and tells Rachael that she will stay there until she decides to resume her duties as cook.

There Rachael remains, starved, the chains chafing her papery old skin. Each time the door to the courtyard opens, she views her granddaughter's grave and hears in her mind the sound of the child hitting the stones. Finally, she can stand it no longer. She stokes up the oven until it is a hellish inferno and sets fire to the house. Rachael means to make her mistress pay, even if it means her own agonizing death.

Neighbors and friends spot the smoke and rush over to help. First they try to pull old Rachael from the kitchen, but it is too late. She screams out the back window for revenge, but the chains hold her fast, and she is consumed by the ravenous flames. She dies, cursing her mistress with her last breath.

New Orleans' Most Famous Murderess Revealed

The rescuers rush into the main house, attempting to pull Madame and Dr. Lalaurie to safety. To their surprise, the couple will not leave. They begin coolly ordering their neighbors to save this treasure and that from their beautiful collection of art and furniture. The fire has consumed the dining room by now, directly above the kitchen chambers.

A house this large does not run itself, and it is common knowledge that Madame bought back her slaves.

"Where are they?" the crowd demands. "Where are the slaves?"

Madame glibly rebuffs them, suggesting that they save a valuable painting instead. She seems as calm and good-natured as she was at her many glittering parties.

Dr. Lalaurie, on the other hand, is flustered and irritable. He, too, refuses to tell the rescuers, including the venerable Judge Canongo, where the slaves are located. He orders his friends and neighbors to mind their own business.

The judge is torn between the rumors he's heard and the respect that the Lalauries' place in society commands. He hesitates and then resumes helping to carry the valuables out of the house.

Soon a New Orleans fire brigade arrives. The men quickly locate an attic room with a heavy padlock. When the firemen demand the key, Madame

Many Creole mansions had attics used to store secrets or old clothes.

claims to have lost it. The strong, competent men break the lock and throw the heavy door open.

They walk into a scene from hell. These men have been on the scene of many a fire and road accident. They have seen plenty of gore in their time. But what they see before them defies description. They might have frozen in horror if it were not for the smell, which pushes them back like a force of nature, causing these strong men to retch and vomit. The smell of death is overpowering, and it is mixed with the foul odors of infection, urine, feces, fear and filthy, unwashed bodies.

They see the grotesque results of Dr. Lalaurie's experiments. The crab woman, the peeled "caterpillar" woman, the sex change couple and the man with the hole drilled into his head, maggots crawling on his face. Some of the victims seem to have been mutilated for no obvious reason at all, the flesh stripped from their buttocks, knees and elbows. The floor is sticky with old blood and slick with puddles of fresh new gore. Buckets of body parts are strewn about the room as casually as if they are baskets of corn. The firemen retreat in horror and nausea.

Madame's nosey neighbor and second cousin, Montreuil, tells Judge Canongo that he knows where there are more slaves. He leads the judge and two others to an attached room.

These are the victims of Madame Lalaurie. Their bodies are scored and striped with the lash. They are starved, concave bellies seeming to touch their own backbones. Some have their mouths and eyes bound with filthy, offal-soaked cloth, presumably to muffle their screams. Some of the chained slaves have been coated with honey. Ants, cockroaches and rats gnaw away at their helpless flesh.

A few of the chained slaves are dead and clearly have been for some time. The rescuers find themselves feeling that the dead slaves are the lucky ones.

The strong men of the New Orleans fire department move in quickly, along with the braver men from the neighborhood. They whisper comfort to the miserable slaves as they unlock their chains.

Some of the slaves die in the attempt to move them. Their poor bodies have taken more punishment than they can bear, and their hearts give out. A few of the slaves have been driven utterly mad. The woman with her limbs broken and reset at horrible angles scuttles into the corner, refusing to let anyone approach her. She lets out a high-pitched, hissing scream whenever a would-be rescuer gets close. Some of the slaves are toxic with infection, burning with fever and ranting. Some cannot seem to pull out of the hopeless terror that has gripped them for so long. One poor soul runs for the attic window as soon as his chains are unlocked. He (sometimes a she in other versions) smashes through the glass and flings himself out the window to his death in the courtyard below.

By this time, the crowd outside the Lalaurie Mansion has grown huge. There is a collective gasp when the first of the pathetic, filth-encrusted, bloody and mutilated slaves is carried from the attic. A few kind souls run and get food for the starved slaves. Only a few of the victims are strong enough to eat, and they immediately howl in pain and perish. The food is too much for their severely deprived bodies.

As these hapless victims are slowly and painfully removed from the room, the crowd's anger grows. Some city officials in the crowd decide that it would be best for the safety of the slaves to take them to the Cabildo,

The Cabildo gate provided a safe haven for the unfortunate victims of the Lalauries. The victims were laid out inside of the courtyard, protected from the mobs trying to view them. *Photo by Victoria Cosner Love.*

some eight blocks from the Lalaurie Mansion. A morbid parade of carnage moves down Royal Street, along Pirate Alley, to the gates of the prison at the Cabildo. There the victims are laid out in the same area where runaway slaves are whipped. The lashes and flails hang on the courtyard wall next to the groaning, bleeding slaves.

The victims remain there for some hours, on display for all of New Orleans to see. More than four thousand people march grimly through the Cabildo to see the poor, wretched souls for themselves.

The huge mob outside the Lalaurie house, a mix of Creoles, black slaves, free people of color and Americans, has never seen anything so horrible. The people howl for the blood of the Lalauries.

Madame is only slightly concerned. She knows that Bastien will be bringing her carriage around for her evening ride momentarily. She can scarcely believe that the mob is so upset about the fate of a few worthless slaves. She smiles and shakes her pretty head in disbelief.

Exactly on time, Bastien arrives in the carriage. Madame steps lightly in and takes her seat, arranging her opulent gown just so. Bastien lashes the horses and begins to shove his way through the crowd.

Evening at St. John's Bayou, circa 1903. *Library of Congress, Prints and Photographs Division, Detroit Publishing Company Collection.*

Ugly, angry faces shout at her from every side. Madame smiles. Whether it is defiance, a lack of empathy or a display of impish and wildly inappropriate humor, she waves at the mob as the carriage gains speed. Soon the carriage is heading down the road to Bayou St. John, where Madame can hire a boat to take her across Lake Pontchartrain, until all of this silliness blows over.

Delphine does not know where her husband Louis is, though she is not concerned about this. Louis is intelligent and cunning. He will find his own way to escape the mob. And if he doesn't, it won't make much difference to her. He was by far her most entertaining spouse, but he is just a husband. He can be replaced. And her children are safe. Delphine arranged to have her daughters and young son taken out through the back of the house while the mob was distracted by her departure.

Madame's carriage arrives at Bayou St. John. Loyal Bastien quickly finds a boat captain and pays him handsomely to take his mistress to the other side of the lake. Madame pats Bastien's cheek fondly and boards the boat. As it paddles into the fog, she can hear the roar of the approaching mob and then the unmistakable shriek of horses in mortal agony. She is almost out of earshot when she hears Bastien begin to scream. She feels a pang for him, as if she has dropped and broken a pretty china music box.

At last the boat makes landing. Madame hires a carriage to take her to the home of a family friend. She is welcomed warmly, given food and drink and a comfortable bed. Sometime during the night, Louis Lalaurie arrives at the house with the children. He is terrified, convinced that the ravening mob will find them at any minute and rip them limb from limb. Madame laughs her tinkling giggle and tells him that he is a silly boy.

While at her friends' house, Madame Lalaurie signs her power of attorney over to her trusted son-in-law. That way, if the ridiculous Americans attempt to press charges against her or seize her assets, she will be protected. Louis Lalaurie does the same.

Madame wonders, however briefly, about her Devil Baby, whom she has never bothered to name. Had he been incinerated in the fire? Had he been pulled from the house by the blood-crazed mob and torn to pieces? She feels wistful for a moment or two. She will miss his shrieks and delightful gibbering, as well as the way he could rip apart a live chicken with his sharp little baby teeth.

Back in New Orleans, after the fire has cooled and the house has been gutted, policemen stay on duty to make sure that no more damage is done to this once beautiful mansion. That very night, they begin to hear scratching and crying coming from somewhere in the house.

The officers and firemen search the devastated mansion for hidden rooms, following the footprint of the house. They search day after day, but no other victims are found. The horrible sounds continue for three weeks before they finally stop.

Rumors begin to circulate that the Lalaurie Mansion is haunted. The dead slaves are already coming back for revenge. The stories whip through the city, growing and changing, becoming more horrific with each whispered retelling. The legend of the most haunted house in America is born.

Madame and Louis Lalaurie know nothing of this. They book passage to Paris as soon as they are able. They have friends and family aplenty there, and they are welcomed with open arms.

From the moment they arrive, they don't lack for food, lodging or fine company. Madame often tells the story of her slight misadventure in New Orleans and laughs about it. The hysterical, crude Americans had made a mountain out of a molehill. Imagine their nerve, chastising a highborn French Creole woman for merely disciplining her own domestics. Her friends and family laugh along with her.

Louis is another matter. He grows more nervous day by day. Much to Madame's irritation, he seems to regret his magnificent and colorful medical experiments. He is becoming a bore, and she seeks the company of other, more interesting gentlemen. One day, Louis packs his trunks and leaves without a word. Madame doesn't miss him in the least.

Her life continues on, one dazzling party after another, until the fateful day when a dreadful American preacher confronts her. He claims to have seen her at her home in New Orleans, torturing her slaves with her own lily-white hands.

Well, this is somewhat embarrassing. Her friends begin to ask her questions she does not care to answer. So Madame retreats to a distant relative's home in Pau, out in the wild French countryside.

Madame Lalaurie enjoys her time there. For the first time in years, she can unleash her bloodlust, even if it is only on foxes and deer. She takes great satisfaction in watching her hounds rip a fox to pieces. It is almost as good as if she had done the deed herself.

Almost.

In December 1842, Madame Lalaurie accompanies her hosts on a hunt for wild boar. Everyone discouraged her from going. Boars can be dangerous, and hunting them is no job for a woman, they insisted. These arguments made Madame Lalaurie all the more keen to see the creature's blood.

The thrill of hot pursuit is overwhelming. She and her horse are right behind the beast. She can smell its fear, and the primal adrenaline rush of blood sport makes her heart pound. Soon she will be close enough to shoot and then, if she is lucky, to plunge her knife into the still-living creature's throat.

But her horse spooks and throws her. She lands hard in the bushes. Before she can catch her breath, the boar spins around and charges. She does not have time to scream before it splits her open from navel to neck. The last thing she sees is her own steaming intestines spilling out on the icy ground. She dies unrepentant, although her agony is overwhelming.

Madame's body is secretly shipped back to New Orleans, as was her wish. She is quietly entombed in the St. Louis No. 1 cemetery in the middle of the night, and there she remains to this day, visited by family who keep the location of her tomb a closely guarded secret.

Do you believe that story?

The authors find it to be about as credible as the plot of any given *Saw* movie. (Lorelei's note: This is not to say that I don't love the *Saw* movies.)

If you want to know what conclusions we have drawn about the Lalaurie affair, turn the page, dear reader.

Chapter 9
Our Conclusions

Ransom Stoddard: "You're not going to use the story, Mr. Scott?"
Maxwell Scott: "No, sir. This is the West, sir. When the legend becomes fact, print
the legend."
–The Man Who Shot Liberty Valance *(1962)*

Did she do it? Was it cruel punishment? Sadistic torture? Was Madame the perpetrator? Was it Dr. Lalaurie? Or was it both?

We believe that, despite a possibly cruel temperament and an impetuous nature that she followed throughout her life, Madame Delphine Macarty López Blanque Lalaurie was not a serial killer, a sexual sadist or a perpetrator of bizarre medical experiments. She was a willful, spoiled, beautiful Creole socialite whose temper led her down the path of infamy. Were slaves abused and tortured at her house on Royal Street? Yes. Was Madame aware of their condition? Almost certainly. But knowing what we now know about her—her passion for surrounding herself with beauty, her avoidance of the unpleasant and her occasional acts of kindness—it seems unlikely that Delphine was the one to get her hands dirty, so to speak.

Exactly how great a role she played in the torture and neglect of the slaves in her household will never be known. Perhaps she gave Louis Lalaurie, or even Bastien, orders to chain people to walls, beat them or break their limbs. Maybe she asked her husband to "discipline" the slaves however he saw fit and looked the other way. It's even possible that Dr. Lalaurie, who had a documented history of physical abuse, committed the atrocities on his own. Perhaps Madame was too afraid of him to stop him, although considering her strong-willed nature, that seems unlikely. Perhaps she did not want to crack the veneer of domestic perfection in her household by attempting to stop the ongoing horrors. Whatever her level of involvement, Delphine Lalaurie was stained with guilt. But we do not believe that she was the legendary monster she has been made out to be. Sadly, the abuse of slaves was not uncommon, even by women. This story from *Harper's Weekly*, July 4, 1863, tells a shocking story of a female slave owner brutalizing her female slave:

Edmund, belonging on the Widow Gillespie's plantation, has been a witness of or knowing to several cases of punishment by the burning process. Two of these were of girls belonging to the Widow G., in New Orleans, and the others occurring on her "island plantation," before referred to. America, wife of Essex, one of the women in the party, related to me the particulars of one case, as follows: There was a middle-aged woman in the family, named Margaret, who had a nursing child. Mrs. Gillespie ordered Margaret to wean the child. The babe was weakly, and Margaret did not wish to do so. Mrs. G. told her that she would examine her breast the next Monday, and, if she found any milk in it, she would punish her severely. Monday came round, and on that day Margaret's stint was to spin eighteen "broaches"—spools—but she did not finish it. At night the promised examination took place, and the breast of Margaret gave but too convincing proof that, in obedience to the yearnings of a mother's heart, she had spurned the threat of the inhuman mistress. Mrs. G. then ordered the handsaw, the leather strap, and a wash-bowl of water. The woman was laid upon her face, her clothes stripped up to around her neck, and "Becky" and "Jane" were called to hold her hands and feet. Mrs. Gillespie then paddled her with the hand-saw, sitting composedly in a chair over her victim. After striking some one hundred blows she changed to the use of the leather strap, which she would dip into the wash-bowl in order to give it greater power of torture. Under this infliction the screams of the woman died away to a faint moan, but the "sound of the whip" continued until nearly 11 o'clock. "Jane" was then ordered to bring the hot tongs, the woman was turned over upon her back, and Mrs. Gillespie attempted to grasp the woman's nipples with the heated implement. The writhings of the mother, however, foiled her purpose; but between the breasts the skin and flesh were horribly burned. During this terrible infliction "Jeems" came out of his room and remonstrated with his mother for "using the niggers so." He "did not wish them punished in that way." Her answer was, "They won't mind me, and I will do with them as I please." Margaret was a long time in recovering from her wounds.

Why is Madame Lalaurie so famous and Mrs. Gillespie forgotten in history, despite better circulation of her story? It may be that the Lalaurie case stood out because the atrocities were committed in the city, inside a home, rather than in the fields. It was easy for the Creole elite to put the brutality of plantation life out of their minds when they did not see it every day. The ongoing cultural struggle between the Americans and the Creoles threw gasoline on the flames. Americans ran many of the papers that covered the incident, and they were only too happy to see a rich, haughty Creole family brought down by scandal. Whatever the reason, Delphine Lalaurie made history.

This in no way excuses the Lalauries for the horrific treatment of their slaves, of course. But the stark, unpleasant reality is that they were no worse than many of their slaveholding contemporaries.

We believe that most of what has been written about the Lalaurie case—including the bizarre medical experiments, the buckets of blood and body parts and the dozens of victims hidden under the floor of the house—is pure myth and invention. We apologize for debunking and deflating a New Orleans legend, but we believe that Madame Lalaurie was, in her own way, a victim, too. She did not suffer the horrors that her slaves did, but she suffered at the hands of an abusive husband, and she was painted as an inhuman monster by the press of the time. This description was perhaps accurate, but if that is the case, almost all plantation owners should be put in the same category. The institution of slavery itself was fundamentally immoral and depraved. It facilitated and even encouraged immoral and depraved acts.

In recent years, the term "serial killer" has been used to describe both Madame and Dr. Lalaurie. No matter what else they were, they did not fit the definition of serial killers.

The term "serial killer" was coined by former Federal Bureau of Investigation (FBI) agent and author Robert Ressler in the 1970s. By his definition, a serial killer is a person who kills three or more victims over a period of more than thirty days, with a "cooling off" period in between. Ressler, in his 1988 work *Sexual Homicide—Patterns and Motives*, attributes almost all serial killing behavior to psychosexual urges. We have no idea if the Lalaurie case was motivated by sexual deviancy, but the Lalauries simply don't fit Ressler's description of serial killers in any other way.

Russian author Peter Vronsky (2004's *Serial Killers: The Method and Madness of Monsters*) has a much broader definition of a serial murder. He includes war crimes, the crimes of slave owners and even institutionalized mass killings of the kind that took place in the ancient Roman Coliseum, referring to the latter as "mass participatory serial murder." That definition could be applied to the entire institution of slavery. Yet the legend of the Lalaurie atrocity still prevails over other true stories of abuse and murder of slaves in the American South.

The fact is that the number of people killed by the Lalauries, if any, is unknown. The stories of the rescued slaves in the attic dropping dead from shock or leaping from the windows are just that—undocumented stories. This is not to say that the Lalauries did not commit murder at any point. But there is no solid documentation to prove that. Surely, if Madame had a history of strange deaths in her home, accidental or otherwise, court documents would have reflected this, and the newspapers would have jumped all over it following the 1834 incident.

The most fascinating aspect of this case is that the story of "Mad Madame Lalaurie" has excited the imagination of the public for so long. This long-standing legend was undoubtedly jump-started by the enormous amount of press coverage it received at the time. Madame's physical beauty and perfect manners may have been the spark that started the flame. It is difficult for modern society to admit that beautiful people, particularly women, can commit the ugliest of acts. In 1830s New Orleans, it was even more shocking to the public. Well-bred Creole women were meant to be the heart of the family and the keeper of the home, never even raising their voices in anger much less committing terrible acts of violence. While other women perpetrated the same kind of abuse, particularly out on the plantations, Madame Lalaurie was the one who got caught.

In the Meigs Frost article from the February 4, 1934 *New Orleans Times-Picayune*, an argument is made for the slandering of Madame Lalaurie by her relative and neighbor, Montreuil.

Montreuil was related to Delphine Lalaurie by the marriage of her aunt, Manette (Marie Marthe), to his uncle. A substantial piece of property reverted to the management of Madame Lalaurie, which resulted in a large loss of income for M. Montreuil. Frost maintains that the reason Montreuil was "all over the place" during the fire is that he was trying to get Madame into as much trouble as possible. He knew of the slaves in the attic and tried to incite as much interest in them as possible.

So Madame was victimized but was probably at least an accessory in the mistreatment of the slaves. What was Dr. Lalaurie's role? If one were to take the legend at face value, including the alleged medical experimentation, he would seem to be the likely perpetrator. The crude sex change operations, the "crab woman" and the victim with the peeled skin go far beyond punishment. These are Nazi-like medical atrocities. Certainly, there are cases and citations of medical experiments being performed on slaves and prisoners, particularly prisoners of color, throughout western history. It was not uncommon for doctors (some with very dubious credentials) to try out new remedies and potions on hapless slaves. But we believe that what was going on in the Lalaurie house was nothing quite so exotic.

Dr. Lalaurie's nonchalant answer to a would-be rescuer of "mind the business at hand" seemed to indicate that he knew what was happening in the locked rooms and was trying to divert attention away from them. But those things were probably not Grand Guignol–style medical atrocities. Those lurid details did not appear in the Lalaurie legend until the 1940s. In fact, they seem to have been inserted by one particular author, Jeanne DeLavigne. It is far more likely that what Louis Lalaurie was trying to hide was a flagrant abuse of power over people whom society had made helpless. Dr. Louis Lalaurie abused his wife—that much was documented in court. A man who would raise his fists to his wife would not cringe at the thought of brutally harming people who were considered to be his property.

In Peter Vronsky's book *Female Serial Killers: How and Why Women Become Monsters* (2007), he stated that the wives and girlfriends of sexual sadists often came from a stable background, had few problems in childhood and were generally well educated. Vronsky cited a 2002 study by Janet Warren and Ron Hazelwood: "The majority of the 42 women studied…lived rather conventional, stable, and non-criminals lives; before the initiation of the relationship that culminated in rather radical changes in their behavior."

As far as we know, Delphine Lalaurie fits that model. There was never a hint of scandal associated with her until she married Louis Lalaurie. Whether he was a sexual sadist is unknown. But someone in that household, maybe both parties, had a wide streak of sadism.

If they were working in tandem, this raises the interesting idea that the Lalauries were enmeshed in the rare psychological syndrome known as "folie a deux," or "a madness shared by two." In more recent psychiatric publications, it's referred to as shared psychotic disorder. Ironically, the syndrome was first postulated in nineteenth-century France, by Drs. Ernest Charles Lasegue and Jules Philip Joseph Falrer.

Simply put, this is a psychotic syndrome in which two people share the same delusion. Sometimes there is a dominant partner who presses a delusional belief on the second. More rarely, two people who have a similar delusion or mental illness meet, and their illnesses feed each other, according to Dr. W.W. Ireland.

One could build a case for this theory. Madame was certainly a strong enough personality to bend other people to her will, whether or not it was rational. And it seems fairly strange that Delphine married Louis after knowing him for only a few months. It's possible, if not likely, that what drew them together was a common bond of madness.

Vronsky describes a study by anthropologist Ilsa Glazer that researched aggression in females (defined as "Masked Criminology") and that showed that "as an offender the woman is perceived as instigating and inspiring violence rather than partaking in it directly." After extensive consideration of the possibilities, we are leaning toward this psychological concept as an answer to what occurred in the Lalaurie Mansion. To put it plainly, we find the most likely scenario to be that the physical acts of torture were committed by Louis Lalaurie, who was encouraged, or perhaps even pushed to action, by Madame Lalaurie.

Another dark twist on this theory is that Madame may have been happy to have Louis' rage turned on someone other than herself. If she encouraged him to torment the slaves, it may have been at least partly an attempt to deflect his abuse away from herself and onto someone else. Not the noblest of motives, but sadly, not uncommon either.

Was Madame Lalaurie mad? Her letters written toward the end of her life indicate a basic lack of understanding of the seriousness of her crimes in New Orleans. In a letter in the collection of the Missouri Historical Society, her son stated the following about Madame Lalaurie's proposal to return to New Orleans in 1842:

> [It is] *a project of which the idea alone is a lack of consideration toward her family. She has been speaking about it in a vague manner but we comfort ourselves with the hope that moments of humor alone could make her nourish a thought that the sad memories of the catastrophe of 1834 must have made her envision as impossible.*

A lack of empathy for victims and a lack of understanding of the gravity of actions is not necessarily indicative of insanity, at least not in the eyes of modern law. A modern western court of law generally judges whether a defendant is insane based on the M'Naghten Rules, created in England by the House of Lords in 1843 following the attempted assassination of the British prime minister, Robert Peel, by an insane individual named Daniel M'Naghten. The M'Naghten Rules read:

> *The jurors ought to be told in all cases that every man is presumed to be sane, and to possess a sufficient degree of reason to be responsible for his*

crimes, until the contrary be proved to their satisfaction; and that to establish a defence [sic] *on the ground of insanity, it must be clearly proved that, at the time of the committing of the act, the party accused was labouring* [sic] *under such a defect of reason, from disease of the mind, as not to know the nature and quality of the act he was doing; or, if he did know it, that he did not know he was doing what was wrong.*

Or, to make a long set of rules short, a person is considered legally insane if he cannot understand that what he did was wrong.

The M'Naghten Rules clearly do not apply to Madame Lalaurie. If she had truly not known that what was being done to her slaves was wrong, she would not have tried to hide that fact by discouraging would-be rescuers from going into the attic. She knew that what she was doing was wrong (or at least illegal). She just did not care.

And then there is the slight possibility that Madame Lalaurie was completely oblivious to the whole situation. Her disobedient slave problems were "taken care of" by her husband. She was absent when the abused slaves were brought forth to the public. She knew that they were being punished. Everyone punished their slaves; why the big fuss? This would account for Madame wanting to return to New Orleans, not realizing the gravity of her husband's sins.

Or perhaps she was a heartless sociopath, which is what we believe to be true.

We believe that Delphine probably suffered from antisocial personality disorder, also known as sociopathy. This is a fairly common personality disorder marked by a lack of empathy and a focus on one's self to the exclusion of the well-being of others. Lacking a conscience, sociopaths do what they want, take what they want and usually get what they want at any cost. They are quite willing to go against social norms to get what they desire or even just to entertain themselves. Most psychiatrists, such as Robert D. Hare, consider this to be a neurological disorder that is often aggravated by trauma early in life.

Sociopaths are superficially charming in the extreme, dazzling others while skillfully manipulating them. They can fit perfectly into any social situation. They are glib, skillful liars, and their true motives often go undetected for years, if not for their entire lives. It's estimated that 1 to 4 percent of the general population are sociopaths, according to Martha Stout.

Sound like anybody we know?

We do not believe that Madame Lalaurie was mad, in the common sense of the word. She was not a drooling lunatic or a paranoid schizophrenic. But her psyche was far from normal. She was the center of her world, and everyone else—slaves, husbands, children, friends and relatives—were just props created for her amusement.

So how much of the legend is true? When you compare the tales found in books, on websites and in the hundreds of tours led through the French Quarter every year to the provable, documented portions of the story, it seems amazing that any of the facts have survived the 180 years of telling and retelling. The core of the story, that Delphine and Louis Lalaurie heinously abused and neglected their slaves, stands true, even if their motives will never be known for certain. Some of the mysteries raised in the tour at the beginning of this book have been explained. Many more are waiting to be solved. The wonderful thing about history is that new facts could turn up at any time—in someone's attic, in a forgotten library storage room, in the basement of a courthouse or in the hope chest of a lady long since passed. Maybe someday we will find something, and we will know more.

Chapter 10
Myths v. Facts

Myth is an attempt to narrate a whole human experience, of which the purpose is too deep, going too deep in the blood and soul, for mental explanation or description.

—D.H. Lawrence

History is the present. That's why every generation writes it anew. But what most people think of as history is its end product, myth.

—E.L. Doctorow

Many of the stories swirling around the Lalaurie legend are provably myths and patently untrue (however entertaining they may be). Here is a rundown of the stories we know to be myths, as well as the truths behind them.

Myth: Madame Lalaurie had two previous husbands who died under mysterious circumstances. Even Louis Lalaurie vanished from public view, and his death date or cause was never established. She may have murdered them, starting and then continuing her career of death and mayhem.

Fact: It's true that there is no documentation for the deaths of any of Delphine's three husbands. But that is hardly unusual, considering that not one of Madame's husbands died quietly at home. Record-keeping and sharing between countries was iffy at best.

She may have been present for one of their deaths. The movements of her first husband, López, are well documented in Cuba with the Spanish governmental papers. If indeed she reached Cuba before he died, he was already very sick while she was pregnant and traveling on a ship to meet him. She did not have the opportunity, or even the motive, to kill him. Few women in the nineteenth century wanted to be left widowed and pregnant.

Jean Blanque's death was not documented (nor was his burial), but his very lifestyle made him almost impossible to track through standard bureaucratic record-keeping of the time. The man was a smuggler, a slave dealer and, quite probably, a pirate. Such men die violently, or they move to faraway countries to spend their ill-gotten gains. The man vanished, one way or another. It is ridiculous to consider that Madame might have murdered him and disposed of his body on her own. No such remains were found at the Blanque home.

Louis Lalaurie and Delphine Lalaurie had been separated from each other for years at the estimated time of his death. Agatha Christie fans might guess that she sent him a poisoned bottle of brandy as a parting gift, but that seems every bit as likely as Madame dragging Jean Blanque's body to the swamp and dumping him herself. In all likelihood, he died in the arms of his "riffraff" family or practicing shoddy medicine in Cuba or Haiti.

Madame Lalaurie's husbands did not die under mysterious circumstances. Not one of them met an end that indicated poison or murder-for-hire, the two most common ways for a woman to dispose of an unwanted husband in the nineteenth century. They did, however, leave her very wealthy. But her own family was very wealthy. Money was simply not a motive for Delphine to murder her husbands, nor was the "shame" of divorce. Divorce was quite common in Creole upper-crust culture, and women were well protected by alimony laws.

Myth: Madame was seen chasing a young slave child through her house, brandishing a bullwhip. She chased the young girl up to the roof, where the child slipped and fell to her death in the courtyard. She was buried next to the well by her grieving relatives.

Fact: No documentation of the death of the slave child exists. If it occurred, this probably would not have been a criminal matter, as most people researching the incident have assumed. If complaints were, in fact, filed by witnesses of the act, the case would have been heard in the civil or parish courts. There are no documents whatsoever indicating that a civil trial took place, much less a guilty verdict handed down.

Most versions of this story claim that Madame was fined and that all of the slaves were removed from her household. No court records can be found indicating that any disciplinary action was taken against the Lalauries or that the case appeared in court at all. No police reports exist to document the event.

During the 1834 coverage of the Lalaurie fire and its horrible revelations in the *Bee* and *Courier*, the editors who dragged Madame Lalaurie through the mud would have been only too happy to bring up any previous problems with her slaves and play them for all they were worth. Yet there was not a single mention of the incident with the unfortunate child. When firemen and police dug up the courtyard, no human bones or bodies were found.

The tale of the murdered child appears in all versions of the Lalaurie legend, but so far, nothing factual has been uncovered that might prove the story to be true.

Myth: Firemen at the scene of the Lalaurie blaze reported horrific and outrageously grotesque scenes of torture.

Fact: This oft-quoted scene is from Jeanne DeLavigne's 1946 book, *Ghost Stories of Old New Orleans*. However, no records were found that involved the firemen documenting or commenting on these atrocities. In fact, the more gruesome and outlandish descriptions—like the extracted and knotted intestines, the people smeared with honey and attacked by ants and the brain stir-sticks—did not appear in the Lalaurie legends until DeLavigne's book was published. This would indicate that these details were either embellishments on the part of that author or perhaps stories that she heard from New Orleans locals who enjoyed spinning a colorful yarn.

The official statement by Judge Canongo indicates that only seven slaves were pulled from the upper galleries and floors of the mansion during the fire. The slaves were not in good condition, and it was determined by rescuers and doctors who examined them at the Cabildo that they had been chained, beaten and starved over a period of some time. As horrible as this is, it is a far cry from intestines pulled out and defleshed joints.

Police records in New Orleans do not go back as far as 1834, and the archives at the state library do not hold any record of the Lalaurie incident. Although photographic equipment existed in the 1830s, it was extremely rare and expensive. It is almost certain that no photographs were taken of the victims of the Lalauries. But newspaper illustrations were quite common,

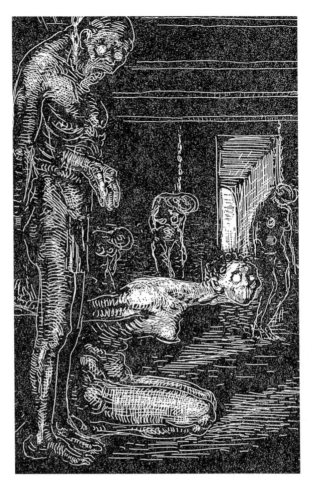

Illustration from Jeanne
DeLavigne's book of
torture victims in the attic.

and these drawings were notoriously lurid. Yet not a single drawing of a slave being devoured by ants or with his intestines wrapped around his abdomen exists. It seems most likely that the "firemen's description" and the stories that sprouted from it, like the "crab woman" and the buckets of blood and guts in the attic, were storytellers' elaborations to make the already shocking tale even more horrifying.

Myth: The story of the hauntings began shortly after the incident, as the ashes cooled and police stayed on the scene to ensure that the structure was not damaged any further. Sounds of whimpers and scratching could be heard, but the firemen and police could not find any more hidden rooms and feared that ghosts were afoot. In the 1970s, when the floorboards of the Lalaurie Mansion were pulled up during restoration, the bodies of up to twenty people who had been buried alive were found.

Fact: Extensive search of newspapers at the time of the '70s restoration did not turn up any stories about bodies being found under the floorboards. No bodies were found during any decades following, either. Had this been an actual event, it would have been huge news, *national* news. But not the smallest paragraph could be found.

Every five to ten years, new articles would show up in the papers about the Lalaurie Mansion, especially around Halloween, but no actual facts about the discovery of bodies emerged from these entertaining articles—just more ghost stories.

The following quote appears in Jeanne DeLavigne's aforementioned 1946 book, *Ghost Stories of Old New Orleans*:

> *Workmen employed to repair the old cypress floors began digging up human skeletons from under the house. The owner of the property, in an attempt to down the mansion's gruesome reputation, announced that the house had been built over an ancient Spanish burying-ground, and that over an Indian graveyard. Which was quite true, only—the bones were too recent to have been deposited there before 1803, and they were too near the surface to have been at any time buried in graves. They were found in all sorts of positions, helter-skelter, some barely covered with soil, shreds of fabric still adhering to some of the bones; and whenever hair was found near a skull, it was Negro hair. Some of the skulls had great holes in them. The authorities said that at least some scraps of wood or metal would have been found with or among the bones, had they been interred in coffins. As they were not in a trench, their burial could not have been in consequence of an epidemic. So it all simmered down to one conclusion—they were bodies of Lalaurie slaves, buried thus in order that their manner of death should not become known.*

It seems likely that the story of the bodies discovered during the 1970s renovation stemmed from DeLavigne's account. But there is no documentation—police reports, newspaper reports or coroner's reports—to indicate that there was a discovery of bodies beneath the floor of the Lalaurie house before the 1970s, either.

Yet again, this would appear to be a colorful yet less-than-accurate horror story from *Ghost Stories of Old New Orleans*.

Myth: Madame and Dr. Lalaurie fled New Orleans the night of the fire. Some stories say that they stayed in Louisiana. Some stories report the appearance of the Lalauries in Mobile, Alabama. Still others believe that they lived the rest of their days out in Paris, where Madame was living in exile and shame. At one point, a preacher recognized her at an estate in the French countryside, and she was forced to flee in the night to avoid discovery.

Fact: It is true that the Lalauries left town that awful night. We have documentation on the Lalauries' flight and much of Madame's life after she fled. Madame resided in Paris for a while and returned to New Orleans for the last decade or so of her life. There is no indication that she was in hiding in France or that she ever tried to hide her identity while there.

Dr. Lalaurie separated from her at some point, and his life after 1842, as well as the date of his death, is undocumented.

Myth: Dr. Louis Lalaurie was experimenting on slaves with "zombie drugs" in order to make them more obedient.

Fact: Just the mention of zombies gives many people a chuckle. Shambling dead people are not exactly in the realm of the possible. But contrary to popular belief, zombies were not invented by George Romero. (Lorelei's note: I love George Romero.)

The word "zombie" (or "zombi") originated in Haiti. Voodoo (or vodu or vodun) is an offshoot of a West African religion practiced throughout the island. There is a common belief among citizens of small villages and rural areas that a voodoo priest has the ability to raise a dead person from his grave and force him to become the priest's slave, according to Dr. Louis P. Mars.

Obviously, that is impossible. But in the early 1980s, a Harvard ethnobiologist named Wade Davis traveled to Haiti to try to discover if there was any truth behind the zombie myth at all. After extensive investigation, he claimed that a living person (not a dead one) could be transformed into a "zombie" by the introduction of two powders into the bloodstream. One is *coup de poudre*, which allegedly contains tetrotodoxin (TTX), which is the poison found in puffer fish. The other powder is made up of a cocktail of dissociative drugs, like those found in the datura (deadly nightshade) family. Supposedly, this combination of toxins produces a deathlike state. The voodoo priest "resurrects" the victim and tells him that he is now a zombie, and the zombie becomes his servant. The "zombie" is known by his stiff gait, his distant stare and his unquestioning obedience of his master, according to Davis.

Toxicologists have disputed the idea that TTX could put a person into a permanent or semipermanent trance. Symptoms of TTX poisoning can range from vomiting to paralysis to death but not complicity or a suggestible trance, according to W. Booth.

However, toxicologists are not taking deeply rooted cultural beliefs into account. If a person is raised to believe that a voodoo priest can bring people back from the dead as his personal slaves, and that person awakens to find himself in a coffin with a voodoo priest telling him he is a zombie, he just might believe he is a zombie. Psychosomatic conditions have caused stranger physical reactions.

Supposedly, Dr. Lalaurie thought that by administering the potion in the proper doses one could get a person to just do what you wanted with no resistance. The downside to this is that the potion used highly toxic ingredients, and if the potion was not prepared correctly it could kill someone. Because the zombie potion recipe is passed on from one voodoo priest to another, there was no exact written recipe to create and administer the stuff. The conclusion one might draw from this information is that Dr. Lalaurie went through many test subjects in his attempt to create the perfect zombie.

If this tale is not wild enough, some people say that Louis Lalaurie was assisted in his experiments by Marie Laveau, the voodoo queen of New Orleans herself. The oral legends say that she brought him her personal enemies to experiment on.

Claudia Williams, a voodoo "queen" currently residing on Royal Street, says that this aspect of the legend is entirely false. But she and her brother both agree that someone who was under the correct dosage of "zombie dust" could be induced to do "just do what they are told."

And what do your humble authors think of all this?

We are open to the idea that people can be drugged and convinced that they are powerless, even dead, particularly in cultures that strongly believe in that possibility. However, there is no proof, nor even a hint that Louis Lalaurie was involved in "zombification" experiments, with or without Marie Laveau—no rumors at the time, no stories of zombies roaming the French Quarter and no mysterious slave poisonings. If he was involved in any kind of medical experimentation on slaves, it would most likely have been related to his work in attempting to cure spinal deformities.

To put it simply, we call baloney on this myth.

Myth: Brought to her by Marie Laveau, Madame Lalaurie stood as the Devil Baby of Bourbon Street's godmother and raised it with the help of her husband, Dr. Louis Lalaurie.

Fact: Looking at this wild and entertaining story, it is easy to dismiss it out of hand as a folktale. But is it possible that there was a grain of truth to the legend? Well, anything is possible.

The Devil Baby story is a classic. A baby deformed, cursed from conception, is taken by the voodoo queen Marie Laveau and raised in the dark, screaming and drooling until the miserable little creature's death. According to legend, Marie Laveau asked Delphine Lalaurie to stand as a godparent for the unfortunate mite. The benevolent Delphine Lalaurie responded that someone had to look after the soul of the grotesque child.

The child allegedly lived five years before the shrieking finally stopped; a family gathering, not including Madame Lalaurie, was seen at the St. Louis No. 1 Cemetery, interring the poor creature.

Let's look at the idea of the baby. Obviously, if it existed, it was not a demon or the spawn of Satan but rather a child with severe birth defects. The description given in stories and the image created by Ricardo Pustanio are similar to what is commonly called a Harlequin baby. This rare birth defect, Harlequin-type ichthyosis, is an extreme thickening of the keratin layer in the baby's skin. This causes huge, diamond-shaped

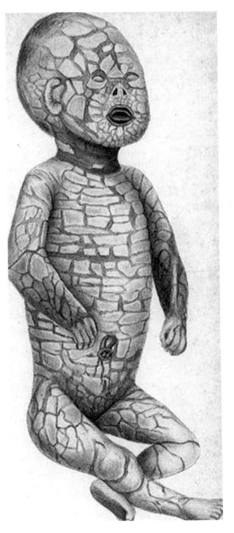

A Harlequin baby medical drawing, 1886. Harlequin-type ichthyosis is a birth defect that may account for what some people referred to as "devil babies."

scales on the baby's body. The spaces in between the scales are an angry red, because the baby's thick skin cracks instead of folding. The constant open wounds on the baby's skin leave it open to bacterial infection and other illnesses.

Harlequin babies also suffer severe facial and cranial deformities, as well as malformed arms and legs. They are susceptible to bleeding and dehydration. The babies are in constant pain, mostly because of the nerves exposed by their constantly splitting skin, according to William James and others.

A Harlequin baby in the 1830s would be extremely unlikely to survive to five years old. Such infants rarely lasted more than a few weeks before they succumbed to some form of systemic infection, exsanguination or dehydration. (As an interesting aside, modern medical science has greatly improved the treatment of children with Harlequin-type ichthyosis. The oldest living survivor is currently twenty-six years old and in good health, according to the *Birmingham Post* newspaper.) And where would Marie Laveau have come up with such an infant anyway?

The details of Laveau's life are shrouded in mystery. Some say that she was a midwife, an abortionist or both. Others say that she ran a brothel at one time. Any of these vocations could have caused Marie to encounter a sadly deformed baby. Marie Laveau was a voodooienne, a highly respected (and feared) voodoo priestess. She was known for her acts of kindness to people in her community, particularly to black and "colored" individuals, whether they were slaves or "free colored." It is conceivable that Marie might have taken pity on such an infant and tried to save it.

Haunted Louisiana's website states that Laveau cursed a couple when the man wanted his wife dead. The curse included the deformed baby, whom she whisked away to use in the future for her own purposes.

Why Delphine Lalaurie would be brought into the story is unknown, other than the fact that Marie Laveau and Madame Lalaurie were arguably the two most interesting women in New Orleans at the time, and any good spinner of tales would find it irresistible to pair them up.

And their meeting is not impossible. Marie was born in New Orleans in 1801, and she died there at the age of ninety-eight in 1881. In the early 1830s, Marie Laveau was a hairdresser to wealthy and privileged Creole ladies. She certainly could have met Delphine at some point. And it is almost certain that Marie Laveau had encountered Delphine's aunts, who lived within blocks of Laveau's beauty shop.

However, Marie's strong suit at that point seemed to be extracting valuable information and gifts of clothing and jewelry from her wealthy

Marie Laveau's tomb in St. Louis Cemetery No. 1. *Photo by Victoria Cosner Love.*

clients. Randomly deciding to hand over a Devil Baby to a highborn Creole lady seems pretty unlikely.

But then there is the wild card of Louis Lalaurie. A physician educated in France, he was interested in physical deformities. At one point, he claimed to have found a cure for hunchbacks. Might he have been interested in a child with a highly unusual birth defect? Almost any doctor with any medical curiosity would be.

But when all is said and done, what is left regarding the Devil Baby story is a lot of hearsay, wild speculation and unlikely coincidences. We do not believe that the story of the Devil Baby of Bourbon Street has any basis in fact, at least not where Madame Lalaurie is concerned. However, we will admit that it's one of our favorite legends connected with the story.

Myth: Madame Lalaurie hated slaves and tortured them because her parents were murdered during a slave uprising in New Orleans or Haiti.

Fact: This is a theory you will often hear from New Orleans ghost tour guides. The story has been bandied about over the years, even in print, like in the May 6, 1975 *States Item*: "Legend has it she tortured slaves to wring from them information about her mother, the fabulous Madam Macarthy, who was murdered on a Carrollton plantation during a slave uprising."

Did Madame hate slaves? There is documentation that she freed a slave in 1819 and another in 1833. Those wouldn't appear to be the actions of someone who hated all slaves on principle. That being said, Delphine's family was affected both directly and indirectly by the Slave Revolt of 1811, and one of her uncles was murdered by two of his own slaves in 1771.

There is a letter written by Barthélémy Macarty to his son-in-law's father, Lebreton, regarding the latter incident:

> *These two Negroes, murderers of their own master, used the cover of night to set fire to the hangard {at the end closest to the mill canal?}. The determined Mirliton, after having appeared at the fire, seeing his master up above in the gallery facing the hangard, gave orders so that the fire would not reach any further point, left the fire to go to the top of the gallery stairs, and from there moved his poor master, who then fell under the shot landed by the cowardly and infamous Dimba, falling on the big lemon tree in the garden...he fired a second shot in case Mirliton had missed.*

This was Delphine's uncle, not her father. It is unknown how close she was to him. An incident like this undoubtedly threw a scare into slave owners and their families throughout the area. But it seems unlikely to have inspired an undying vendetta against all slaves in Delphine. There was, in fact, a bloody uprising in 1811 outside of New Orleans. Jean François Trepagnier, Delphine's first cousin, was one of two documented deaths of whites during the uprising. Again, Delphine's relationship with her cousin is unknown, although losing a family member was probably frightening and unnerving. An extremely romanticized telling of Jean François' stand against the marauding slaves was written at the time. This story depicts him as a valiant defender against evil, which was the popular perception of the whites killed in the uprising at that time. It's likely that Delphine shared that opinion.

The other death also had a Delphine connection. He was Gilbert Andry (or Andre), whose niece, Felicite Amanda Andry, would marry Delphine's son, Jean Pierre Paulin Blanque. One of her aunts married into the Andry family as well, making it a close connection for Madame. However, the later matchup did not happen until after 1850.

The uprising marched along the German coast of the Mississippi and could conceivably have reached the Macarty plantation. It was stopped only two plantations away. It was reported in the local paper that women and children in the path of the angry slaves were fleeing for the safety of town. But there is no documentation whatsoever that Delphine's parents were killed in this uprising.

The slaves responsible for organizing the 1811 uprising were captured and slaughtered in a frenzy of brutality.

One slave uprising that does not have a comprehensive list of victims is the Haitian Revolution. This was the first documented slave rebellion that actually succeeded, resulting in a free Haiti run by a government of former slaves.

The Haitian Revolution was bloody and brutal, as all revolutions are. However, we have not found any documentation, or even a story or rumor, that Delphine's mother was tortured and killed in this slave uprising, or any other. In fact, Delphine's mother's death preceded the Haitian Revolution by at least twenty years. Her father's death is documented in New Orleans in 1846.

There is no evidence that Delphine lost anyone close to her in the Haitian Revolution. Even if she had, torturing her probably American-born slaves for information more than twenty years later, in the 1830s, doesn't make a lot of sense.

We have no way of knowing what was in Delphine Lalaurie's head when she tortured her slaves or allowed her husband to torture them. But these authors do not believe that any kind of grudge or vendetta was involved. The Lalaurie atrocities appear to have been more a crime of opportunity and oppression than revenge.

Myth: Madame Lalaurie died in France in about 1840 after being gored by a wild boar during a hunt.

Fact: This is a great story, but it just isn't true. There is no telling how this tale got started, but it sounds like wishful thinking on the part of someone who wanted to see Madame get her just desserts. It must have been comforting for some people to think that, even if she escaped the justice of the court, she died horribly on the tusks of a savage beast.

Myth: Madame Lalaurie died in 1842 and is buried in the St. Louis Cemetery No. 1.

Fact: There was a plaque found in the 1940s in St. Louis Cemetery No. 1, Aisle 1, bearing the name of Madame Lalaurie and showing a death date of 1842. Although the plaque was real (there is a photograph of it), there is no guarantee that it was authentic. We have proven that she died sometime between 1855 and 1858.

A house in the French Quarter similar in style to the way 1140 Royal Street would have appeared in 1830. *Photo by Victoria Cosner Love.*

New Orleans' Most Famous Murderess Revealed

Myth: The Lalaurie Mansion was rebuilt after the fire to its original plan.

Fact: Sadly, the building gazed upon by modern tourists is not the design of the house the Lalauries purchased. It was renovated extensively after the fire of 1834. Both contemporary reports and historical documents show that the house was a two-story, Creole-style mansion in the 1830s The current, three-story house is in the style of the 1840s and 1850s. The Williams Research Center has documents verifying both the contemporary reports and the original structure.

Myth: Firemen and police heard scratching and moaning coming from the house for twenty-one days after the fire, but they were unable to find anyone. The haunted stories thus began. In the 1970s, the floorboards were replaced, and bodies were found, with evidence that they had been buried alive.

Fact: As early as 1858, there were reports that no bodies were found in the well or on the property. No newspaper or court records show the discovery of bodies in the 1970s.

Myth: The Lalaurie Mansion is the most haunted building in New Orleans.

Fact: Discover that truth or myth for yourself.

Chapter 11
And What About the Haunted House?

I t's all about the haunted house, isn't it? That is why people visit the epicenter of the legend—they're hoping to see a ghost. Website after website suggests that the hauntings are well documented and prolific. The quotes to the press are endless, and interviews with residents seem to ring eerily true.

Unfortunately, in this day of TV shows like *Ghost Hunters* and *Most Haunted Places*, no one has been allowed access to the Lalaurie Mansion to investigate with modern ghost hunting equipment. And why is that? One reason cited by two paranormal societies is that the last owner, actor Nicolas Cage, is hard to contact and that the realtor handling the property needs permission from the owner to let anybody in. (As of October 2010, the house had been on the market for almost a year until Mr. Cage recently lost it due to financial difficulties, carrying on the theme of the house bringing bad luck to its owners.)

Located in what is now the Sixth Ward, this house has mesmerized people for nearly two hundred years. After the Lalaurie estate sold the house, a long and bumpy ride of tenants, businesses and private owners paraded through and were usually driven out by the alleged hauntings and happenings. The history of the house is a testament to the power of the Lalaurie legend. On Google, you only have to type in "New Orleans Haunted House," and you get the Lalaurie Mansion. You can almost always find postcards on eBay of the "Haunted Lalaurie Mansion," as well as the Warrington House, a school for wayward boys that the mansion housed in the 1920s and '30s. These images are of the iconic three-story building from the now famous catty-

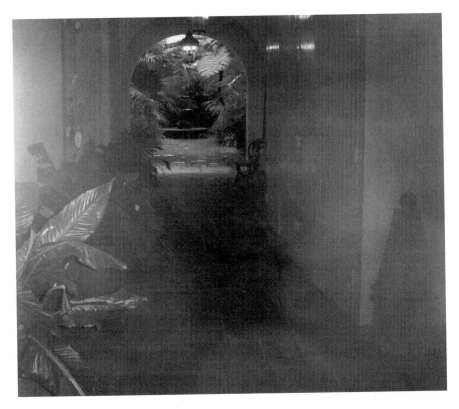

Above: Thousands of people return from New Orleans with photographs that have ghostly qualities. Even the authors succeeded in capturing orbs. *Photo by Victoria Cosner Love.*

Right: The Warrington House, circa 1930. For a while, the cursed house was home to wayward boys and men, primarily those who were no longer able to be handled by their families. Historic postcard. *Authors' collection.*

corner angle across the street from the house. The postcards range from turn of the twentieth century to the 1950s.

As the Lalaurie Mansion was sold to one owner after another, the tales of hauntings grew and changed, building on the stories that had come before. In the years immediately following the fire, the widespread belief that the place was haunted was enough to keep the superstitious from walking by the house after nightfall.

Most of the following was organized from websites and articles about the mansion.

THE LALAURIE HOUSE AND ITS ALLEGED HAUNTINGS: A TIMELINE

1831: Madame Delphine Lalaurie and husband, Dr. Louis Lalaurie, buy the house at 1140 Royal Street from Edmond Soniat du Fossat. The house was constructed as a two-story, Creole-style house with an enclosed courtyard. The galleries along the rear of the house were used as slave quarters, and the rest of the house was living area for the owners.

1833: Rumors spread about Madame Lalaurie's cruelty to her slaves. She is allegedly seen whipping a child slave on the roof of the house before the young girl falls to the courtyard and is killed instantly.

1834: A fire breaks out at the house, allegedly started by a female slave chained in the kitchen. (Some versions of the story say that this woman is the slave child's grandmother.) Rescuers discover tortured, starved slaves locked and chained in rooms in the attic. The slaves are taken to the Cabildo, and anger at their horrifying state spreads as fast as the fire. A mob gathers and destroys the house. Only parts of the exterior walls are left. All furniture and movable goods are stolen or destroyed.

Firemen and policemen supposedly report hearing scratching and moaning in the house but are unable to locate anyone. The rumors of the hauntings begin.

The Lalauries escape New Orleans and sign their business affairs over to Auguste Delassus. He maintains their property until he sells it in 1837 through the city.

Pirate Alley, where victims of the Lalauries were taken to enter the Cabildo for safekeeping. *Photo by Victoria Cosner Love.*

1837–1865: The house is rebuilt in its current three-story configuration and purchased in 1837 by a man who only keeps it for three months. He tells friends and family that the house plagued him with awful noises, cries and groans in the night and that he was driven to flee the place. He tries leasing the rooms, but the tenants only stay for a few days at most. Finally, he gives up, and the house is abandoned once again.

The house is rented out. A furniture store occupies the basement for a short time. The house is a barbershop for a few months. No tenant or business stays there very long. It is rumored that there is a curse on the location and that no endeavor can or will succeed there.

1860–1865: The Civil War rages throughout the country. During Union occupation, it is rumored that the Lalaurie house plays a part. The 1938 *New Orleans City Guide* claims that "[d]uring the years of the Civil War the house was used as Union headquarters." (We have been unable to verify that General Butler used the Lalaurie Mansion as his headquarters.)

Circa 1872: During Reconstruction, the house becomes a public high school "for girls of the Lower District." This school enrolls both white and black students. New Orleans is more open to desegregation than the rest of the South, but a great deal of prejudice remains, simmering beneath the surface. In 1874, the White League forces the black children to leave the

GEN: BUTLER HOLDING THE MOB IN CHECK AT NEW ORLEANS.

General "Beast" Butler ruled occupied New Orleans during the Civil War, quelling negative public taunting by enacting a law that proclaimed that if a woman insulted a U.S. soldier, she would be legally considered a prostitute. Legend has it that he lived in the Lalaurie Mansion, but this has not been verified. *Library of Congress, Prints and Photographs Division.*

school. The vigilantes line the girls up and question them about their family backgrounds in an attempt to discover who is "colored" and who is not. (The children's races are not always immediately obvious. Some of the mixed-race girls are more fair than some of the "whites.") Girls determined to be "colored" are forcibly removed from the school.

1873: The house is listed as a leaf tobacco business owned by Joseph Barnes. However, according to the 1938 *New Orleans City Guide*, "in the 1870s the building became a gambling-house. Stories were told and retold of the strange lights and shadow objects that were seen flitting about in different apartments, their forms draped with sheets, skeleton heads protruding. 'Hoarse voices like unto those supposed to come only from the charnel house floated out on to the fog laden air on dismal and rainy nights, with the ominous sound of clanking chains coming from the servant's quarters where foul crimes are said to have been committed.'"

1876: The May 28, 1876 *Daily Picayune* runs an article about the house being up for auction. It is described as "admirably adapted for a large boarding school, asylum, a first class boarding house or spacious summer residence. The building is leased for the summer renting at the rate of $150 per month."

1878: The New Orleans school system is officially segregated. The house becomes a high school for black girls only. The school lasts for one year.

1882: The mansion is turned into a "conservatory of music and fashionable dancing school." The owner is a well-known English teacher, and the school thrives with students from the finest local families. Shortly before a grand recital, a local newspaper apparently prints an accusation against the owner, claiming staff improprieties with female students. As the owner stands outside, dressed in formal evening wear, students and guests shun the place. The school closes the following day.

That night, it is rumored that the spirits of the Lalaurie house hold a wild carnival to celebrate their triumph.

An interesting note is that the school's manager, W. Warrington, later buys the house and establishes the Warrington House for wayward boys.

1889: An apartment in the house is occupied by Joseph Edouard Vigne for a little more than three years. Neighbors believe that he is a poor, crazy man. Vigne keeps to himself.

1892: Vigne is found dead upstairs. According to rumor, black crepe is seen on the doors of the house. An inspection of Vigne's apartment reveals more than $10,000 in cash and family heirlooms stashed in various places around the dwelling. The contents of the house are auctioned off. No one admits to hanging the black crepe.

1893: According to the June 4, 1893 *Times Democrat*, "F. Greco purchased the haunted house at Hospital and Royal…yesterday he posted large flowing placards upon the walls of the building announcing in both Italian and English, 'The Haunted House.' There is an end to everything, so there is with ghosts. Come and be convinced. Admission ten cents."

Circa 1900–1923: The house changes hands five times in twenty-three years. Castellanos stated, "A year or two ago, it was the receptacle of the scum of Sicilian immigrants, and the fumes of the malodorous filth which emanated from its interior proclaimed it what it really is."

In this time of mass immigration to America, many Italians come to live in New Orleans. Landlords quickly buy up old and abandoned buildings to convert into cheap housing for this new wave of renters. The Lalaurie Mansion becomes such a house. But for many of the tenants, even the low rent isn't enough to keep them there.

Jeanne DeLavigne cited this period as the first occurrence of bodies being found under the floor: "Workmen employed to repair the old cypress floors began digging up human skeletons from under the house…So it all simmered down to one conclusion—they were bodies of Lalaurie slaves, buried thus in order that their manner of death should not become known."

As compelling as this account is, there is no other documentation to back it up, such as from police reports or newspaper articles.

1920: The house is a tenement by this time. There are many reports of ghosts. "There were no other families living here and one night, on the third floor, I saw a man walking carrying his head on his arm," reported one resident. Another resident saw a large black man wrapped in chains on the main stairs, confronting an Italian tenant. The chained man disappeared on the last step. A young Italian mother found the apparition of a wealthy white woman bending over her sleeping baby. The ghostly woman was later identified as Delphine Lalaurie herself. In some versions of the story, Delphine is attempting to suffocate the infant.

1923: The mansion is bought by William Warrington, and it becomes the Warrington House for wayward boys until 1932. Warrington House is listed in the 1930s *Soards' New Orleans City Directory* under "Hospitals and Sanitariums." The Warrington House would last a full eleven years before closing. William J. Warrington had up to thirty "madcap" boys in his custody at any given time. Many of these children had first been sent to the parish prison before they were released into Warrington's care.

The lack of paranormal activity reported during the Warrington House's decade in business is interesting, especially considering that many paranormal researchers believe children to be more sensitive to the supernatural than adults. Perhaps the rowdy, noisy boys were too much for the Lalaurie house ghosts, and they retreated into seclusion until the lively lads were gone.

1932: The house is sold to the Grand Consistory of Louisiana. (A consistory is an organization that confers the degrees of the Ancient and Accepted Scottish Rite of Freemasonry.) The consistory sells the house in 1942. Whether the house ghosts and the Freemasons got along is unknown.

Circa 1945: The house becomes a bar. Taking advantage of the building's ghastly history, the proprietor calls the place the Haunted Saloon. The owner knows many of the building's ghost stories, and he keeps a record of the many strange things seen and experienced by his patrons. (Of course, reports of floating objects and blurry figures must be taken with a grain of salt during this time, considering that the reporters may have had multiple shots of bourbon under their belts.)

Circa 1950s: A furniture store opens but does not do well at this location. The owner first suspects vandalism when all of his merchandise is ruined and found in the morning covered with a foul, unidentifiable liquid. The merchandise is replaced and is ruined again, more than once. One night the owner waits in the store with a shotgun, hoping to catch the vandals in the act. At sunrise, he finds the furniture befouled again. He closes the store for good shortly thereafter.

Historic photograph of the Haunted Saloon, circa 1945. *Authors' collection.*

1964: The house stands empty. An article in the *Times-Picayune* dated April 17, 1964, reports that a preservation group, the Vieux Carré Commission, is trying to stop the deterioration and partial demolition of the house at 1140 Royal Street. Evidently, people had been looting the abandoned house down to its very bones. The preservation group reported that "the building has been stripped of floor boards in the upper balcony," among other things. The thieving and vandalism had been going on for some thirty-eight months.

1969: Zella Funck—artist, resident of the haunted house and "ghost host"—is interviewed by the *New Orleans States Item* reporter Laurraine Goreau for her column "C'est la vie." Funck says that her "poltergeists are just playful. They're not around every day, but they do surprise visitors."

She describes an incident where a cat was seen in the room of a guest who did not believe in spirits. Funck did not own a cat. She also describes one of her ghosts as a "romantic figure of a man. I've watched him for several minutes in a full-length mirror before he faded away. He's about 5'9", about 170 lbs, has a reddish clipped beard, and wears a creamy beige felt hat turned up slightly, with a cord around it."

She ends the article with a story about her doors opening by themselves. "Contact," she says, "usually comes when I'm sitting by the window, where Madame's husband is said to have had his desk…I can tell you one thing positively. I've never heard clanking of chains."

A person who believes in ghosts might wonder if the handsome man she spotted was, in fact, Louis Lalaurie.

Circa 1970–2000: The house is divided into about twenty apartments before it is purchased by a retired New Orleans physician. He restores the home to the state he believed to be original but was actually the second design of the house. It includes a living area in the front portion and five apartments to the rear of the building. He has no paranormal experiences while living in the house. Perhaps Dr. Lalaurie left him alone out of professional courtesy.

During the 1970s renovation, the second round of rumors about bodies being found beneath the floorboards crops up. There is no documentation to prove this or even suggest that it is true.

2007: Actor Nicolas Cage buys the property and is said to be living in one part of the house and renting out apartments along the gallery, where the slave quarters were located.

2008: The Lalaurie Mansion is back on the market at a price of $3.5 million.

2009: Cage loses this and two other New Orleans haunted houses due to delinquent taxes. Regions Financial Corporation purchases the foreclosed property for $5.5 million on November 13, 2009.

2009: Claudia Williams—self-proclaimed voodoo priestess and proprietor of Starling Magickal Books and Crafts, located on Rue Royal, three blocks from the Lalaurie Mansion—asserts that the house is no longer haunted: "I have spent time outside the house enough to know that I have never had a sense that there was anything ghostly happening there."

She also emphatically states that the house is back to its original configuration, which sadly is not true. The *New Orleans Bee* reported on April 12, 1834:

> *The whole of the edifice is demolished and scarcely any thing remains, but the walls. Whist the popular vengeance have consecrated with various writings expressive of their indignation and the justness of their punishment. The loss of property sustained is estimated by some as $40,000, but other think that is exaggerated. It must, however, have been very great indeed.*

The article goes on to report about fine furniture and decorations being thrown from the garrets to the street, "rendering them of no possible value, whatsoever." Martineau relates, two years later, that people slashed feather mattresses from the house and that the streets were covered with down, making them treacherous to walk on for some time.

Later visitors, including Cable and other early authors who wrote of the Lalaurie story, did not know that the house had been substantially altered. But does rebuilding and transforming a house chase away its ghosts? Not the ghosts of memory, obviously.

A haunting, at least at the date of this writing, is impossible to prove or disprove. You can wave all the electromagnetic field meters and recordings of supposed electronic voice phenomena in the world at a full-blown skeptic, and he will never believe you. Show him a photograph of a "ghost" and he'll say it's a smear in the emulsion.

Conversely, shower a believer with scientific facts and rational explanations for seemingly supernatural phenomenon, but if that person truly believes in ghosts—especially if he feels that he's had a firsthand encounter with one—he will not be swayed from his beliefs.

There are plenty of people who believe that they've encountered ghosts and the supernatural within the walls of the Lalaurie Mansion.

We, too, have stood outside this gorgeous structure, hoping to see something or feel something, anything. We came away disappointed. All we saw was a quiet, beautiful fortress with an evil history. If the hair stood up on the back of our necks, it was because we were thinking of the horrors that took place in the Lalaurie Mansion. We heard not a ghostly whisper, not a muffled cry.

Certainly the house deserves its share of ghosts. It has been so many things: home to the infamous Lalauries; the site of an integrated school whose children were victim to a racial uprising; a miserable, wretched Italian tenement; a school for men with learning disabilities. If houses do, in fact, retain traces of their owners, or even the remnants of human energy, the Lalaurie house should be humming with ghostly emanations. So much emotion, so much suffering. This house represents the rise and fall and rise of this historic neighborhood, the struggle between the old French Creole ways and the new Americans, as well as the rich racial history of the Vieux Carré.

We have no way of knowing if this house is, or ever was, haunted. But we do know that the Lalaurie house is irrevocably associated with murder, torture and unrest. The tour guides who show the Lalaurie house over and over again are well versed in New Orleans history. They are also storytellers of the finest caliber. Each guide these authors have had the honor to meet has put a slightly different spin on the Lalaurie story.

Add up the stories, the documentation, the cultural times, women's roles and expectations, the decline of the Creole culture, the rise of the Americans, yellow journalism, voodoo, torture, family ties and money… and you have a legend. Now stir in the wilder stories: ghastly medical experiments, devil babies, haunted portraits and zombification drugs. Or consider the dreadful idea proposed by our tour guide for Haunted New Orleans Tours: the practice of dumping slaves in the swamps when they died as a viable way for the Lalauries to have practiced fatal experiments on a huge number of victims.

Multiply all of this by the thousands of visitors to New Orleans who have gone home and retold the story to horrified, fascinated friends and family, and you get the makings of a legend larger than life. This legend transcends almost two hundred years, kept alive by thousands of ghost tours dedicated to the perfect ghost story, all starring the Mad Madame Lalaurie.

Delphine's Thoroughly Impressive Legacy and Family Connections

An ounce of blood is worth more than a pound of friendship.
—*Spanish proverb*

To look at Delphine's family connections, both up and down her family tree, is to take a trip through the history of New Orleans. Her family had its hand in banking, the industry of merchants, pirating, slave trading, sugar cane, cotton and politics, as well as in the very foundation of New Orleans. Although there were some dubious characters and black sheep in the family (one can't describe piracy or the slave trade as particularly admirable occupations), Delphine is the only member of the clan associated with torture, murder or insanity.

Here are some of the famous and venerable families connected to Madame Delphine Lalaurie.

ANDRY

Gilbert Andry (or Andre) was a plantation owner whose niece, Felicite Amanda Andry, married Delphine's son, Jean Pierre Paulin Blanque. The marriage took place in 1850 or so, long after the scandalous events at the Lalaurie Mansion. Andry's plantation lay along the route of the Slave Revolt of 1811, and he was killed in the uprising. He became a hero in local folklore, which described Andry as standing on the plantation house balcony and defending his home to his last breath, armed with only a sword.

Another, older connection to the Andry family also exists. William DeBuys (son of Gaspard) married Corrinne Andry (daughter of Gilbert). Their son, William DeBuys, married Adele Marie Macarty, Delphine's cousin.

DE BIENVILLE

Jean-Baptiste Le Moyne de Bienville was the founder of the city of New Orleans. He led the way for French colonization of the area with more than twenty years of military service, establishing forts. He repeatedly served as governor of French Louisiana and established a dynasty that supported Louisiana's and New Orleans' massive growth during the eighteenth and nineteenth centuries.

Jean D'Estrehan married Genevieve Bienville (granddaughter of Jean-Baptiste), binding the mighty Desteran family to the Macartys by marriage. Jean's daughter, Elanore D'Estrenhan, married Edourard Macarty—Delphine's second cousin—connecting the Macartys to the very beginning of New Orleans.

LE BRETON DES CHAPELLES

Jean Baptiste Césaire Le Breton des Chapelles married Jeanne Françoise de Macarty, Delphine's aunt. He was one of the French king's own bodyguards, a Mousquetaire Noir. Jean Baptiste held the office of commandant of militia at the German coast and held the rank of captain in the Spanish army, according to Stanley Clisby Arthur.

Le Breton des Chapelles was murdered by two of his slaves on what would later become the Macarty plantation. Several documents about his death have survived, including a court paper describing the torture used to obtain the slaves' confession and a letter from Delphine's father to Jean Baptiste's father about the murder.

DEBUYS

According to family history, the DeBuyses were one of New Orleans's oldest French Creole families. The DeBuyses adjusted well to the changing governments of Louisiana, and they made a substantial fortune. Gaspard

DeBuys served as a member of the first legislative council of Louisiana and served under General Jackson during the Battle of New Orleans. One of the DeBuys descendants was one of the architects who designed the main quadrant of Loyola University. William DeBuys (son of Gaspard) married Corrinne Andry (see prior section). Their son, William DeBuys, married Adele Marie Macarty, Delphine's cousin.

DELASSUS

Charles de Hault Delassus was the last Spanish lieutenant governor of Upper Louisiana. He oversaw the transfer of the territory to the Americans on March 9–10, 1804. Ironically, he was not Spanish himself, but French. He was born in Bouchaine, Flanders, on November 17, 1767, and joined the Spanish army when he was fifteen. By 1794, Delassus had risen to the post of lieutenant colonel in the elite royal battalion of King Charles IV of Spain, the Royal Walloon Guards. When the French Revolution broke out, Delassus's parents fled to America and settled in Upper Louisiana. Soon they were destitute and appealed to their son for assistance. Delassus resigned his commission and asked for a transfer to the Louisiana Regiment so that he might be near his family.

In 1833, Marie Louise Jeanne Blanque (called Jeanne) married Pierre Auguste de Hault Delassus, son of Charles de Hault Delassus. Pierre Auguste (1813–1888) was the only son of Charles de Hault Delassus and Feliciana Martina Leonardo Delassus. Auguste, as he was known, was born in New Orleans on July 4, 1813. In 1833, he married Marie Jeanne Blanque (1815–?). They had six children.

Auguste Delassus was closely associated with Delphine Lalaurie. Delphine transferred her power of attorney to him before she and her husband fled New Orleans. Delphine repeatedly wrote to him from France, complaining about the state of her financial affairs. It is in letters to Auguste Delassus that Delphine voiced her desire to move back to New Orleans.

Auguste died at his home in Delassus on January 15, 1888. His body was taken to St. Louis and buried in Calvary Cemetery.

Destrehan

Jean Baptiste Destrehan (name appears variously throughout historical texts) was the royal treasurer of French Louisiana colonies and was a man of great wealth and power in New Orleans. He purchased a humble cottage and its surrounding lands and then had it torn down and replaced with a suitably fine home for his family.

His son, Jean I. Destrehan, built Destreran Plantation, located on the German coast of the Mississippi. This plantation is famous for being the place where the Louisiana Slave Revolt of 1811 was quelled.

A tribunal court was set up to punish the leaders of the slave rebellion and the slaves from the Destreran plantation who participated. All of those convicted suffered horrendous fates.

The Desteran plantation is one of a few premier remaining examples of the French Creole architectural style.

Jean Destrehan married Genevieve Bienville (of the New Orleans founding family), binding the Destrehan family to the Macartys by marriage. Jean's daughter, Elanore D'Estrenhan, married Edourard Macarty, Delphine's second cousin.

Forstall

Borquita, Delphine's daughter by her first husband, married Françoise Placide Forstall, the son of an old French family. His grandfather, Nicholas Michel Forstall, was appointed for four terms, from 1774 to 1801, as the first alcalde (judge of the first instance) of New Orleans.

Françoise's father, Edmond Forstall, was one of the most influential members of the family. From 1832 until he died in 1872, he held the New Orleans agency of Hope and Company of Amsterdam and the Baring Brothers of London. He used these to negotiate the sale of bonds issued by the state. He was also one of the front people involved in framing the law for the incorporation of free banks in Louisiana.

A revolutionary sugar-refining apparatus was invented by a young man of mixed race named Edmond Rilleux. Edmond Forstall is cited as one of the first people to import and use one of the new sugar-refining machines. These were expensive machines, and some of the smaller plantation owners were unable to afford them. But further innovations eventually lowered the cost.

Forstall was shipping refined sugar in the early 1830s to New York. Edmond Forstall contracted Rilleux's father to build one of the machines at the Louisiana Sugar Company, but something went wrong with the contract and a bitter feud flared up. Rilleux disappeared, and Forstall canceled his contract with him. This cost the Forstall family millions of dollars—the refining process invented by Rilleux revolutionized the sugar industry.

Lanusse

Paul Lanusse was one of the leading merchants in the city of New Orleans until his business failed. In 1804, he served on the board of directors of the newly established State Bank of Louisiana. He was elected an alderman in 1812. Paul was married to Marie Céleste Macarty, Delphine's aunt. Marie Céleste's sister, Mitilde, married Charles Lanusse. This fact caused many confusing moments, because quite a few of the early historians did not realize there was a double liaison with the families. Charles Lanusse comes up in Gayerré's histories, but Paul seemed to be the one who consistently stayed in the spotlight.

The Lanusses were prominent in business and politics. Paul Lanusse was one of the judges who decided on the fate of the slaves found guilty of insurrection in the Slave Revolt of 1811. It was Paul who sued the infamous pirate Pierre Laffite (Jean Laffite's brother) for monies owed to him—a total of about $9,000. This suit would eventually lead to Pierre Laffite's arrest.

De Montreuil

The neighbor who was present while the slaves were pulled from the burning Lalaurie house was a Montreuil. The Montreuil family dates back to the days of Norman dominancy in French history. Marthe Macarty (one of Delphine's fabulous aunts) married Gaultier de Montreuil. This union produced a landownership war that resulted in hard feelings between the Monsieur Montreuil (Delphine's cousin) and the Macartys. It was this Montreuil who witnessed the Lalaurie fire and passed along information about the mistreatment of the Lalauries' slaves. One news writer, Meigs Frost, theorizes that the rumors of abuse and perhaps even the story of the little murdered slave girl, Nina, may have been Montreuil's invented or embellished revenge on Delphine's family for taking land from his coffers.

Marigny de Mandeville

A litany of the Marginys' contributions to society, family connections and money is listed in Grace King's book *Old Families of New Orleans*. The Marigny plantation hosted the exiled princes of France in 1798 during the French Revolution. The Marignys threw lavish parties for their royal guests, spawning stories of the family's extravagance for generations. The princes' host, Pierre Phillipe Marigny, held connections in Creole society to almost every powerful family, including the Macartys. Marriage alliances tied the two families as in-laws.

Historian Stanley Clisby Arthur, in his book *Old Families of Louisiana*, noted:

> *It was the third child of Phillipe Bernard Xavier de Marigny de Mandeville (son of Pierre Phillipe) who represented the family during the last century; and who is the hero, par excellence of New Orleans' social traditions; who, we may say was to the Marigny family what the final bouquet is to a pyrotechnic display.*

This young man is credited with bringing the game of craps from Europe to Louisiana, setting the standards of 1820s fashionable extravagance and his loss of the family's lands and fortune.

Miró

Esteban Rodriguez Miró (1744–1802), governor of Spanish Louisiana from 1785 to 1791, married Céleste Éléonore de Macarty, Delphine's aunt.

Miró arrived in Louisiana at the beginning of the Spanish ownership of the territory and was a primary figure during the Spanish occupation.

In 1785, Miró became governor of Spanish Louisiana. Miró passed one of the first slave codes that restricted slaves from ownership of firearms and the ability to travel, as well as provided for several other provisions. During his appointment, the fire of 1788 burned a large part of the city, and Miró was primarily responsible for rebuilding many of the structures still in existence in New Orleans, including the Cabildo and the St. Louis Cathedral.

His Macarty bride, Céleste Éléonore Elisabeth, is noted in *Old Families of New Orleans* as "young, beautiful and all Irish by her quick wit."

Grace King stated:

New Orleans had never been so gay as under her husband's or rather her administration with the opera, theatre, balls, card parties and pleasure jaunts to the suburb of Bayou St. Jean or across the river to the plantation of her aunt, Madame Jonchere.

When Miró put in for retirement, "he left Louisiana not only reconciled to Spain, but even endeared to it and beautified by its domination," according to King.

After Miró passed away, his wife was so despondent that she begged her niece, the Baroness de Pontalba, to come live with her in Paris. The baroness did, taking her son, Tonton, and leaving her husband to write an incredible journal of the Creole royalty in New Orleans.

PELLERIN

Delphine's grandfather, Barthélémy, married Françoise Hélène Pellerin. Françoise's father, Gerard Louis Pellerin, was first to command the Opelousas/Attakapas Post settled in 1720, located on the banks of the Bayou Tech. The Attakapas Territory was nestled between the Atchafalaya River and the Bayou Nezpique and was populated by the eastern Attakapas tribe. This area eventually became the community of St. Martinsville and a haven for the ousted Acadians and other French immigrants.

DE PONTALBA

Delphine's cousin, Jeanne Françoise Le Breton des Chappelles, married Joseph Delfau de Pontalba. Joseph, the Baron de Pontalba, left a wonderful journal that he wrote to his wife, who joined her aunt, the Widow Miró, in France.

De Pontalba's main contribution to history is his spectacular journal and the letters kept and sent to his wife after she and their son went to stay with Madame Miró. Beautiful descriptions of Creole life are found in these writings.

Rathbone

Marie Jeanne "Céleste" Forstall, Delphine's granddaughter, married Henry Alanson Rathbone, continuing the Rathbone dynasty. The Rathbones were one of Rhode Island's founding families. Henry Alanson Rathbone arrived in New Orleans after the War of 1812. Grace King regarded him as "one of the few Americans that was received with distinction in Creole Society."

Regarding Henry's wife, Céleste (née Macarty), King wrote that she

> *retained her beauty to old age. Her stately home on Esplanade Avenue, surrounded by a great garden, maintained its standard of old fashioned elegance and its luxurious appointments, long after the Civil War, which ended the old standards of living as the old Regimé.*

Trepagnier

In 1718, a French Canadian named Claude Trepagnier joined Bienville's expedition party that carved out Ville de la Nouvelle Orléans. As a reward for his participation in the expedition, Claude Trepagnier was granted a plot of land. In 1721, when the official design of the city was laid out, the grid pattern of the streets of the new town was centered at the Place d'Armes, now known as Jackson Square. The central focus of the traditionally designed French town was the St. Louis Cathedral, which was part of the Trepagnier land grant, making it a key plot of land.

In 1735, Claude's daughter, Marie Françoise, made her second marriage to Jean Baptiste Macarty, making her Delphine's aunt.

During the Louisiana Slave Revolt in 1811, Charles Gayerré narrated the encounter between Jean-François Trepagnier (Delphine's cousin by marriage), a planter, and the attacking mob of slaves. When the shouts of the mob alerted the planter of their arrival, Trepagnier loaded his shotgun with buckshot and faced them from "a high circular gallery which belted his house." Jean François Trepagnier is one of two confirmed white deaths from the Slave Revolt of 1811.

VILLERÉ

Jacques Phillippe Villeré (April 28, 1761–March 7, 1830) was the second governor of Louisiana after it became a state. He was the first Creole and the first native of Louisiana to attain that office. In 1784, Villeré married Jeanne Henriette de Fazende (Delphine's cousin), the daughter of Gabriel de Fazende, who owned a plantation seven miles downriver from New Orleans in Saint Bernard Parish.

In 1815, he was elected governor of Louisiana. He took office the following year and served through 1820. His governorship marked a period of diversity, economic gain and population growth for Louisiana.

King finished her chapter on the Villerés with the following: "[T]he Villerés count more descendents in active business life in the city than any other of the 'foundation families' as they may be called."

Authors' Notes

We chose to standardize the spelling of "Macarty." It has at least three different forms during the family's history. Putting the pieces together is always difficult; there were many conflicts in even the genealogy of the families. We hope that we pieced it together fairly accurately but apologize for any mistakes. In regard to other standardizations of last names, we generally used the spelling that was found in documents relating closest to the 1834 time period.

If some of the history contradicts itself, that is what history does. We tried to be consistent in facts, spellings and anything else we could control, but let's face it—this is why history is fun.

Lastly, we halfheartedly apologize for taking the wind out of the ghost legend. Madame Lalaurie is a fascinating character who transcends more than just being a ghost. She is the personification of the change in New Orleans, the role of women, the perception of women's personas, race relations, myth, history and colonial French and early American history, as well as so much more. On top of that, the ghost story is a treasure to those of us interested in the other world: dazzling, powerful families; serial-killing wives; zombies; devil babies; torture; gore; sex; race; eyewitness testimony; and genteel façades. It doesn't get better than this.

Glossary

abolitionist
A person who wanted to end slave trade and emancipate all slaves.

arpent
A common unit of length used in the 1830s. It measured 191.944 feet, or 58.504 meters.

bayou
A body of water in a flat, low-lying area. Sometimes a bayou is a slow-moving river or stream and sometimes a swampy or marshy lake.

black
In colonial and early American Louisiana, the term "black" was used only in reference to people from Africa or of full-blooded African ancestry.

black gold/black ivory
Illegal slave traders referred to their cargo of slaves as black gold or black ivory.

bondsman
In colonial and early American Louisiana, the term "bondsman" was used interchangeably with the term "slave."

caballero
A Spanish knight, often a horseman.

Cabildo
1. The building that housed the seat of colonial French and Spanish government in New Orleans, Louisiana.
2. The group of men who made up the Spanish municipal government in colonial Spanish Louisiana.

caleche
A horse-drawn carriage with a folding hood.

chevalier
A French knight, often a horseman.

Code Noir
France's adopted code of conduct in regard to slaves. A similar code was adopted by Louisiana and kept after it became part of the United States.

coup de poudre
A powder said to be part of the drug used by Haitian voodoo priests to turn victims into "zombies."

Creole
The original definition of Creoles is used in this book: people who were white residents of Louisiana, born of old French or Spanish families.

datura
A flowering plant belonging to the family *Solanaceae*. The tropane alkaloids (toxins) found in datura are said to be part of the recipe for creating "zombie powder."

Faubourg Marigny
A neighborhood in New Orleans.

folie a deux
From the French for "a madness shared by two," a rare psychiatric syndrome in which two people share the same delusion.

Grand Guignol
The Grand Guignol was a theater in Paris known for performing naturalistic, gory horror shows. The term is currently used to mean anything excessively gruesome and bloody.

Harlequin baby
A baby suffering from Harlequin-type ichthyosis.

Harlequin-type ichthyosis
A severe skin disease characterized by a thickening of the keratin layer, producing huge, diamond-shaped scales on the body.

intendant
A supervisor appointed by the Spanish Crown to manage the treasury and the collection of taxes and promote economic growth in a particular area, such as a Spanish colony.

M'Naghten Rules
A set of rules written by the British House of Lords in 1843 and meant to define whether or not a person is mentally fit to stand trial for a crime.

mulatto
A person with one parent who is African or of African descent and one white parent. Outdated.

octoroon
Someone who has at least one great-grandparent who was African or of African descent. Outdated.

person of color
In colonial and early American Louisiana, the term referred to someone of mixed African and white ancestry. Outdated.

piastres
A unit of currency. It was originally equal to one silver dollar or peso and served as the major unit of currency of French colonies.

privateer
A pirate operating on behalf of a government.

quadroon

A person who has at least one grandparent who is an African or of African descent. Outdated.

sadism

A personality disorder in which a person takes pleasure or amusement in humiliating or physically harming another.

sociopath

An individual with a personality disorder marked by a lack of empathy. Sociopaths lack a conscience and generally do whatever they want, regardless of the consequences to others.

Vieux Carré

Literally "Old Square"; the original city was planned around the Vieux Carré, which is now commonly known as the French Quarter.

voodoo/vodou/vodu/vodun

A religion brought to Louisiana by West Africans, vodun eventually merged African gods with Catholic saints to create a unique faith.

zombie

According to Haitian tradition, a zombie is a dead person brought back to life and enslaved by a voodoo priest. Many people today believe that zombies are actually drugged (but indisputably living) individuals whose will has been crushed by a toxic combination of powders.

zombie dust/zombie powder

A combination of toxins said to have the ability to turn a person into a "zombie"—a mindless, utterly obedient servant. Zombie dust is said to contain *coup de poudre*, a powdered form of puffer fish toxin and a strong dissociative drug like those found in datura.

Bibliography

Alvord, Clarence Walworth, and Clarence Edwin Carter, eds. *The Critical Period 1763–1765*. Vol. 10. Collections of the Illinois State Historical Library. Springfield: University of Illinois, 1915.

Arthur, Stanley Clisby. *Old Families of Louisiana*. New Orleans, LA: Harmanson Publisher, 1931.

———. *Old New Orleans: A History of the Vieux Carré, Its Ancient and Historical Buildings*. New Orleans, LA: Harmanson Publisher, 1936.

Benfey, Christopher. *Degas in New Orleans: Encounter in Creole World of Kate Chopin & George Washington Cable*. Berkeley: University of California Press, 1997.

Booth, W. "Voodoo Science." *Science* 240 (1988): 274–77.

Buman, Nathan A. "To Kill Whites: The 1811 Louisiana Slave Insurrection." Master's thesis. Louisiana State University, Agricultural and Mechanical College, August 2008.

Burgess, Ann W., John E. Douglas and Robert K. Ressler. *Sexual Homicide: Patterns and Motives*. New York: Free Press, 1995.

Burnside, Scott, and Alan Cairns. *Deadly Innocence*. New York: Grand Central Publishing, 1995.

Cable, George W. *The Creoles of Louisiana*. Gretna, LA: Pelican Publishing Company, 1884, 2005.

———. *The Grandissimes*. Whitefish, MT: Kessinger Publishing, 2004.

———. *Strange but True Stories of Louisiana*. New York: Penguin Publishing Company, 1994.

Castellanos, Henry C. *New Orleans As It Was: Episodes of Louisiana Life*. Gretna, LA: Pelican Publishing, 1990.

Clay, Henry, James F. Hopkins, Mary W.M. Hargreaves and Robert Seager, eds. *The Papers of Henry Clay*. Lexington: University Press of Kentucky, 1973.

Clisby, Arthur. *Old New Orleans*. Gretna, LA: Pelican Publishing, 1936.

Cochran, Estelle M. Fortier. *The Fortier Family and Allied Families*. San Antonio, TX: self-published, 1963.

Conrad, Glenn R., ed. *The German Coast: Abstracts of the Civil Records of St. Charles and St. John the Baptist Parishes, 1804–1812*. Lafayette: Center for Louisiana Studies, University of Southwestern Louisiana, 1981.

Conroy, John. *Unspeakable Acts, Ordinary People: The Dynamics of Torture*. New York: Alfred A. Knopf, 2000.

Darkis, Fred R., Jr. "Madame Lalaurie of New Orleans." *Louisiana History* 23, no. 4 (Fall 1982).

Davis, Carol Anne. *Women Who Kill: Profiles of Female Serial Killers*. London: Allison & Busby, 2007.

Davis, Wade. *The Serpent and the Rainbow: A Harvard Scientist's Astonishing Journey into the Secret Societies of Haitian Voodoo, Zombis, and Magic*. New York: Simon & Schuster, 1997.

Davis, William C. *The Pirates Laffite: The Treacherous World of the Corsairs of the Gulf.* Orlando, FL: Harcourt Press, 2005.

Deiler, John Hanno. *The Settlement of the German Coast of Louisiana and the Creoles of German Descent.* Philadelphia, PA: Americana Germanica Press, 1909.

Delassus–St. Vrain Family Collection, 1544–2001. Missouri Historical Society Archives, St. Louis, Missouri.

De Laussat, Pierre Clement. *Memoirs of My Life to my son during the Years 1803 and After, Which I spent in Public Service in Louisiana as Commissioner of the French Government for the Retrocession of France of that Colony and Its Transfer to the United States.* Baton Rouge: Louisiana State University Press, 1978.

DeLavigne, Jeanne. *Ghost Stories of Old New Orleans.* New York: Rinehart and Company, 1946.

Douglas, John, and Mark Olshaker. *The Anatomy of Motive: The FBI's Legendary Mindhunter Explores the Key to Understanding and Catching Violent Criminals.* New York: Pocket, 2000.

Duffy, John, ed. *Rudolph Matas' History of Medicine in Louisiana.* Vols. 1 and 2. Gretna, LA: Pelican Publishing, 1976.

Dwyer, Jeff. *Ghost Hunter's Guide to New Orleans.* Gretna, LA: Pelican Publishing Company, 2007.

Engerman, Stanley, Seymour Drescher and Robert Paquette, eds. *Slavery.* New York: Oxford University Press, 2001.

Farrington, Karen. *Dark Justice: A History of Punishment and Torture.* New York: Smithmark Publishers, 1996.

Forbes, Robert Pierce. *The Missouri Compromise and Its Aftermath: Slavery and the Meaning of America.* Chapel Hill: University of North Carolina Press, 2007.

Forster, Elborg, and Robert Forster, eds. *Sugar and Slavery, Family and Race: The Letters and Diary of Pierre Dessales, Planter in Martinique, 1803–1856.* Baltimore, MD: Johns Hopkins University Press, 1996.

French, B.F. *Historical Collections of Louisiana: Embracing Translations of Many Rare and Valuable Documents Relating to the Natural, Civil, and Political History of that State.* New York: D. Appleton, 1851.

Gayerré, Charles. *History of Louisiana.* New York: William J. Widdleton, 1867.

Geneovese, Eugene D. *Roll Jordan, Roll: The World the Slaves Made.* New York: Vintage, 1976.

Gordon, Christopher. "Finding Madame Lalaurie." *Le Journal* 22, no. 4 (Fall 2006). Center for French Colonial Studies.

Gould, Robert Freke. *Gould's History of Freemasonry Throughout the World.* Vol. 5. New York: Charles Scribner and Sons, 1936.

Groom, Winston. *Patriotic Fire: Andrew Jackson and Jean Laffite at the Battle of New Orleans.* Ann Arbor: University of Michigan Press, 2006.

Hambly, Barbara. *Fever Season.* New York: Bantam, 1999.

Hare, Robert D., PhD. *Without Conscience: The Disturbing World of the Psychopaths Among Us.* New York: Guilford Press, 1999.

Hornblum, Allen M. *Acres of Skin: Human Experiments at Holmesburg Prison.* New York: Routledge, 1999.

Howe, Samuel Gridly. *Letters and Journals of Samuel Gridley Howe: Edited by his Daughter, Laura E. Richards…with Notes and a Preface by F.B. Sandborn, V1.* Boston: Dana Estes and Company, 1906.

Hunt, Lynn. *Inventing Human Rights: A History.* New York: W.W. Norton & Company, 2008.

Ireland, W.W. *Folie à Deux: A Mad Family.* New Orleans, LA: Williams Research Center, Historic New Orleans Collection, 1998.

James, William, Timothy Berger and Dirk Elston. *Andrews' Diseases of the Skin: Clinical Dermatology.* 10th ed. St. Louis, MO: Saunders, 2005.

BIBLIOGRAPHY

John Macarty and Family Papers, 1764–1935. Special Collections, Hill Memorial Library, Louisiana State University.

Kelleher, C.L., and Michael D. Kelleher. *Murder Most Rare: The Female Serial Killer*. New York: Dell, 1999.

Kendall, John. *History of New Orleans*. Chicago, IL: Lewis Publishing Company, 1922.

King, Elizabeth Grace. *Creole Families of New Orleans*. 1st ed. New York: MacMillan, 1921.

Kirwin, Barbara R. *The Mad, The Bad, and the Innocent: The Criminal Mind On Trial—Tales of a Forensic Psychologist*. New York: Little, Brown & Company, 1997.

Kukla, Jon, ed. *A Guide to the Papers of Pierre Clement Laussat: Napolean's Prefect for the Colony of Louisiana and of General Claude Perrin Victor*. New Orleans, LA: Historic New Orleans Collection, 1993.

Louisiana Court of Probates (Orleans Parish), Louisiana Division/City Archives, 1805–1846.

Louisiana Division, City Archives. Biography and Obituary Index, New Orleans Public Library.

———. News Indexes, New Orleans Public Library.

Louisiana Parish Court (Orleans Parish), Louisiana Division/City Archives. Index to Slave Emancipation Petitions, 1814–1843.

———. Index to Suit Records, 1813–1846.

Mars, Louis P., MD. "The Story of Zombi in Haiti." *Man: A Monthly Record of Anthropological Science* 45, no. 22 (1945): 38–40. Journal of the Anthropological Institute of Great Britain and Ireland.

Marshall, Mary Louise, ed. *Rudolph Matas History of the Louisiana State Medical Society*. Vol. 1. New Orleans, LA: Rudolph Matas History of Medical Trust Fund, 1957.

Martineau, Harriet. *Retrospect of Western Travel in 2 Vols.* London: Haskell House Publisher, 1969.

McCarty, William F. "The Chevalier Macarty Mactigue." *Journal of the Illinois State Historical Society* 61, no. 1 (Spring 1968).

McCoy, Alfred. *A Question of Torture: CIA Interrogation, from the Cold War to the War on Terror.* New York: Holt Paperbacks, 2006.

McKelvey, Tara, ed. *One of the Guys: Women and Aggressors and Torturers.* Berkeley, CA: Seal Press, 2006.

M'Naghton's Case, House of Lords, 10 Cl. & F. 200, 8 Eng. Rep. 718 (1843).

Patsalides, Beatrice. *Ethics of the Unspeakable: Torture Survivors in Psychoanalytic Treatment.* New York: Après-Coup Psychoanalytic Association, 1960.

Patterson, Benton Rain. *The Generals: Andrew Jackson, Sir Edward Pakenham, and the Road to the Battle of New Orleans.* New York: New York University Press, 2005.

Peña, Christopher G. *General Butler: Beast or Patriot, New Orleans Occupation, May–December 1862.* Bloomington, IN: AuthorHouse, 2003.

Rodriguez, Junius P., ed. "German Coast Uprising (1811)." *The Encyclopedia of Slave Resistance and Rebellion.* Westport, CT: Greenwood Press, 2007.

Seebold, Herman de Bachelle, MD. *Old Louisiana Plantation Homes and Family Trees.* Gretna, LA: Pelican Publishing Company, 1971.

Sitterson, J. Carlyle. *Sugar Country: The Cane Sugar Industry in the South, 1753–1950.* Lexington: University of Kentucky Press, 1953.

Smith, Kalila Katherina. *Journey into Darkness: Ghosts, Vampires of New Orleans.* New Orleans, LA: De Simeon Publication, 2004.

Stampp, Kenneth M. *The Peculiar Institution: Slavery in the Ante-Bellum South.* New York: Alfred A. Knopf, 1956.

Stout, Martha. *The Sociopath Next Door*. New York: Broadway Publishing, 2006.

Thrasher, Albert, ed. *On to New Orleans! Louisiana's Heroic 1811 Slave Revolt*. 2nd ed. New Orleans, LA: Cypress Press, 1996.

Toledano, Roulhac, and Mary Louise Christovich, with photographers Betsy Swanson and Robin Von Breton Derbes. *New Orleans Architecture: Faubourg Treme and the Bayou Road: North Rampart Street to North Broad Street Canal Street to St. Bernard Avenue*. Gretna, LA: Pelican Publishing Company, 2003.

Vronsky, Peter. *Female Serial Killers: How and Why Women Become Monsters*. New York: Berkley Books, 2007.

———. *Serial Killers: The Method and Madness of Monsters*. New York: Berkley Trade, 2004.

Walk, Alexer, and Donald J. West, eds. *Daniel McNaughton: His Trial and the Aftermath*. London: Royal College of Psychiatrists Publications, 1977.

Wansell, Geoffrey. *An Evil Love: The Life of Frederick West*. London: Headline Publishing, 1997.

Washington, Harriet. *Medical Apartheid: The Dark History Experimentation on Black Americans from Colonial Times to the Present*. New York: Doubleday, 2006.

Whitaker, Arthur Preston. *The Mississippi Question, 1796–1803: A Study in Trade Politics & Diplomacy*. New York: American Historical Association, 1934.

Williams, Claudia. *Haunted Space—Public Places*. New Orleans, LA: Starling Publications, 2004.

Zimpel, Charles F., engraver. *Topographical Map of New Orleans and its Vicinity, Embracing a distance of twelve miles up and eight and three quarters miles down the Mississippi*. Circa September 4, 1833. Hand-colored engraving. New Orleans, LA: Historic New Orleans Collection.

INTERVIEWS

Barbian, Lenore, professor of forensic anthropology, Edinboro University, Pennsylvania. Personal interview, November 2009.

Pustanio, Ricardo, artist. Phone interview, September 2009.

Taylor, Annie, Louisiana Paranormal Society. E-mail interview, October 2009.

Williams, Claudia, voodoo priestess and owner of the Starling Magickal Books and Crafts. Personal interview, January 2010.

NEWSPAPER COVERAGE

Frost, Meigs. "Was Madame Lalaurie of Haunted House Victim of Foul Plot?" *New Orleans Times-Picayune*, Sunday, February 4, 1934, magazine section.

Goreau, Laurraine. "C'est la Vie." *New Orleans States Item*, June 16, 1969.

Griffin, Thomas. Unnamed column. *New Orleans States Item*, March 7, 1966.

New Orleans Bee. April 11–12, 1834.

New Orleans Daily Picayune. "Auction by Palfrey and Hill." May 28, 1867.

New Orleans States Item. June 16, 1969.

New Orleans Times-Picayune. "Quarter Group Urges Action." April 17, 1965.

———. "Relic Found Here Revives Legend of Mme. Lalaurie." August 9, 1964.

New York Times. "The Recent Duel in New Orleans." April 29, 1870.

WEBSITES

BlackPast.org. Remembered and Reclaimed. http://www.blackpast.org.

Creole History. "1808 New Orleans Map/Property Owners." www.creolehistory.com/1808_map/prop_owners.html.

Delphine Lalaurie Haunted Mansion House, New Orleans, Louisiana. http://hauntedneworleanstours.com/lalaurie.

Haunted America Tours. "Madame Delphine Lalaurie." http://www.hauntedamericatours.com/hauntedhouses/lalauriemansion/lalaurie.

The Lalaurie House. http://www.prairieghosts.com/lalaurie.html.

Mad Madame Lalaurie. http://www.mad-madame-lalaurie.com.

Milestone Documents. www.milestonedocuments.com.

National Park Service. "French Creole Architecture." www.nps.gov/history/nr/travel/louisiana/architecture.htm.

———. "More Information on Charles Dehault Delassus." The Lewis and Clark Journal of Discovery. www.nps.gov/archive/jeff/LewisClark2/circa1804/StLouis/BlockInfo/Block6CCharlesDelassus.htm.

New Orleans Ghosts. http://www.neworleansghosts.com/haunted_new_orleans.htm.

New Orleans Ghost Tour. http://neworleansghosttour.com.

New Orleans Haunted Houses. www.hauntedhouses.com/states/la/new_orleans_hauntings.cfm.

University of Pennsylvania. "Dead Space: St. Louis Cemetery No. 1." Historic Preservation Program. http://cml.upenn.edu/nola.

———. "Preserving New Orleans' Cities of the Dead." Historic Preservation Program. http://cml.upenn.edu/nola/pdfs/NOLASATpr0902.pdf.

Unsolved Mysteries. "Mme. Delphine Lalaurie and the Lalaurie Mansion." http://www.unsolvedmysteries.com/usm383823.html.

About the Authors

Victoria Cosner Love has spent the better part of thirty years poking around graveyards and digging for lost pieces of history. She is especially fond of delving into missing pieces of women's history. She coauthored a book, *Women Under the Third Reich* (Greenwood Publishing), and now has turned her attention to the infamous Madame Lalaurie and

Victoria Cosner Love (right) and Lorelei Shannon at the House of Blues in New Orleans.

her incredible family. A longtime member of the Association for Gravestone Studies, she has worked in public history facilities for more than twenty years and has her master's degree in American studies, specializing in cultural landscapes of garden cemeteries.

Lorelei Shannon has spent the better part of thirty years following Victoria Cosner Love around graveyards for her own inscrutable purposes. Lorelei and Victoria met at the tender age of fourteen. From the very start they shared a love of history—particularly the obscure and unusual variety. While Victoria went on to become a respected historian, Lorelei became a novelist. She never lost her love of history, and she frequently incorporates historical elements in her southern gothic fiction. This is her first book-length work of nonfiction and her first collaboration with Victoria. She hopes it will be the first of many.

Visit us at
www.historypress.net